ANCIENT RELIGION
AND
MYTHOLOGY

THE DIONYSIAC MYSTERIES
OF THE HELLENISTIC
AND ROMAN AGE

Martin P[ersson] Nilsson

ARNO PRESS

A New York Times Company

New York / 1975

Editorial Supervision: ANDREA HICKS

———◆———

Reprint Edition 1975 by Arno Press Inc.

Copyright © by Svenska Institutet i Athen
Reprinted by permission of
  Martin P. Nilsson's dödsbo

Reprinted from a copy in
  The Swarthmore College Library

ANCIENT RELIGION AND MYTHOLOGY
ISBN for complete set: 0-405-07001-2
See last pages of this volume for titles.

Manufactured in the United States of America

———◆———

Library of Congress Cataloging in Publication Data

Nilsson, Martin Persson, 1874-1967.
  The Dionysiac mysteries of the Hellenistic and
Roman age.

  (Ancient religion and mythology)
  Reprint of the 1957 ed. published by C. W. K.
Gleerup, Lund, Sweden, as no. 5 of Skrifter utg. av
Svenska institutet i Athen, 8°.
  1. Dionysia. I. Title. II. Series.
III. Series: Svenska institutet i Athen.
Skrifter : Acta, Series altera ; 5.
BL820.B2N5   1975   292'.9   75-10643
ISBN 0-405-07261-9

SKRIFTER UTGIVNA AV
SVENSKA INSTITUTET I ATHEN

ACTA INSTITUTI ATHENIENSIS REGNI SUECIAE

8°, V

MARTIN P. NILSSON

THE DIONYSIAC MYSTERIES
OF THE HELLENISTIC AND ROMAN AGE

THE DIONYSIAC MYSTERIES
OF THE HELLENISTIC
AND ROMAN AGE

BY

MARTIN P. NILSSON
PROFESSOR EMERITUS OF CLASSICAL ARCHAEOLOGY AND
ANCIENT HISTORY IN THE UNIVERSITY OF LUND

L U N D
C W K GLEERUP
1957

This book is published with a grant
of the Humanistic Foundation

Printed in Sweden

Copyright by Svenska Institutet i Athen

LUND 1957
SKÅNSKA CENTRALTRYCKERIET

Miscellanea.

Corrigendum.

In my book, The Dionysiac Mysteries of the Hellenistic and Roman Age, p. 93 f., I have made a mistake which is annoying, although it does not affect my argumentation. Miss CHRISTINE ALEXANDER, Curator of the Greek and Roman Antiquities in the Metropolitan Museum in New York, has kindly called my attention to it. She writes: »May I in passing call attention to an unimportant misunderstanding on Dr NILSSON's part, on his pp. 93 ff? The cup fig. 22 a, b is not in New York. CUMONT's »New York», which understandably misled M. P. N., refers simply to the place of publication. This cup or mould, rather, since the photograph is from a plaster impression, actually does have the altar scene, and the fluting satyr as well, i. e., all the figures shown in the Florence cup, NILSSON's fig. 21. The real New York mould is CVA, U. S. A., fasc. 9, Met. Museum, Fasc. 1, plates 2—4, and it too has all the figures, but in another sequence. All this does not affect his arguments, but he might like to correct it for a future edition.»

P. 53, line 1 some words have been omitted in the inscription quoted. It reads: τὸν ἐκ τῆς διατάξεως μύστην ἐπιμεληθέντων τῶν περὶ τὸν Καθηγεμόνα Διόνυσον μυστῶν.

Lund.   *Martin P. Nilsson.*

CONTENTS

Illustrations.

Abbreviations
of Collections of Inscriptions.

BMI	Greek Inscriptions in the British Museum
CIG	Corpus inscriptionum graecarum
CIL	Corpus inscriptionum latinarum
IG	Inscriptiones graecae
I Magn.	Inschriften von Magnesia am Mäander
I Perg.	Inschriften von Pergamon
IG Rom.	Inscriptiones graecae ad res Romanas pertinentes
Kaibel	G. Kaibel, Epigrammata graeca e lapidibus collecta
LS	Leges graecorum sacrae e titulis collectae, ii: l, ed. L. Ziehen
LSAM	F. Sokolowski, Lois sacrées de l'Asie mineure
OGI	Orientis graecae inscriptiones, ed. W. Dittenberger
Peek	W. Peek, Griechische Vers-Inschriften, i, Grabepigramme
Quandt	Gu. Quandt, De Baccho ab Alexandri aetate in Asia Minore culto, Diss. philol. Halenses, xxi:2
SEG	Supplementum epigraphicum graecum
SIG	Sylloge inscriptionum graecarum, ed. W. Dittenberger, 3rd ed.

My book, Geschichte der griechischen Religion, is cited as GGR.

ACKNOWLEDGEMENT.

I wish to express my warmest thanks to Professor Francis R. Walton of the Florida State University who has gone through my manuscript, improving my English style, and. read the first proofs. Certain inconsistencies fall to my account.

I. Introduction.

Much has been written and discussed about the Oriental mysteries, and the great religious change in Late Antiquity has even been imputed to them. Far less attention has been paid to the Dionysiac mysteries, though they too were very popular and widespread. This is understandable. Little is known of their content, and their religious ideas have seemed not to be of great importance. The literary testimonies are few and scarce, while the principal sources that do exist fall into two separate and unconnected groups: inscriptions from Asia Minor and the neighbouring countries, and secondly, monuments of art, chiefly from Italy. A new stimulus to research was given by the discovery in 1909 of the magnificent frescoes in the Villa Item near the Porta Ercolanense at Pompeii.[1] Professor Rizzo tried to interpret the representations and prefaced his study with a chapter in which he collected a number of other monuments representing the initiation of a child into the Bacchic mysteries. He took it to be the child Dionysos.[2] This chief monument has been treated repeatedly and interpreted variously. We shall come back to it at length below. In the last edition of his famous book on the Oriental religions in Roman paganism Cumont added an appendix on the Bacchic mysteries in Rome,[3] in which he tried to show that they were influenced by the Oriental religions. In spite of my reverence for the great scholar I am bound to state that this is a mistake. Of course Dionysos was venerated in the Orient and identified with some Oriental gods, but this has not affected his mysteries in Greek and Roman lands. In the section which Cumont devotes to the Bacchic mysteries in his

---

[1] Published for the first time by G. de Petra, Notizie degli scavi, 1910, pp. 139 ff., with 20 plates. See further p. 66 n. 1.

[2] G. E. Rizzo, Dionysos Mystes, Accad. di archeologia etc. di Napoli, 1915, pp. 39 ff., with many relevant illustrations and good plates of the frescoes.

[3] F. Cumont, Les religions orientales dans le paganisme romain, 4th ed., 1929, pp. 195 ff.

posthumous work he does not come back to this idea.[4] Father
Festugière has written an article on the Dionysiac mysteries.[5]
The first chapter is a substantial survey of the associations and
their organization, the second is a critical account of Orphism.
Here the origin of the Zagreus myth is ascribed to the third
century B. C. and it is said to be a copy of the Osiris myth:
Orphism, he says, had no influence on the Dionysiac mysteries.
At that time the inscription from Smyrna, treated at length
below, was not known. Jeanmaire ended his book on Dionysos
with a chapter on the Hellenistic and Roman age, in which he
distinguishes between the old and the new forms of the Bacchic
mysteries and especially tries to bring out the political implica-
tions of the latter.[6] The most recent contribution is Bruhl's book
on the Italian god Liber pater.[7] Of course the author was bound
to pay attention also to the Greek god with whom Liber was
identified, Bacchus. He has a chapter with the title: Bacchus
dans l'art décoratif de Pompéi et de Rome, a rather superficial
survey of the monuments in which he shows little interest in
their interpretation. The subject of the book is the cult in
general, not the mysteries. He gives an account of its history in
Late Antiquity in Rome and the Western provinces. The cult
of Bacchus was popular in Africa, and this is treated at some
length by G. Picard.[8] The cult and the mysteries of Dionysos
are touched upon in many other books and papers; here I have
mentioned only the principal works.

I have myself repeatedly come back to the Dionysiac mysteries
of this age. I commented upon the great inscription of Agripi-
nilla in the Metropolitan Museum,[9] I inserted a few pages on

---

[4] F. Cumont, Lux perpetua, 1949, pp. 250 ff.

[5] A.-J. Festugière. Les mystères de Dionysos, Revue biblique, xliv, 1935, pp.
192 ff. and 366 ff. Survey of the Dionysiac associations in F. Poland, Geschichte
des griechischen Vereinswesens, 1909, pp. 196 ff.

[6] H. Jeanmaire, Dionysos, 1951, pp. 417 ff.

[7] A. Bruhl, Liber Pater, origine et expansion du culte dionysiaque à Rome et
dans le monde romain, 1953, Bibl. des écoles franç. d'Athènes et de Rome, vol.
175.

[8] Gilbert Picard, Les religions de l'Afrique antique, 1954, pp. 194 ff.

[9] En marge de la grande inscription bacchique du Metropolitan Museum, Studi

the Dionysiac mysteries in my history of Greek religion,[10] I wrote papers on Dionysos Liknites,[11] on the Bacchic mysteries of the Roman Age,[12] and on a new inscription from Smyrna.[13] If a third volume of my Opuscula Selecta, containing papers published after 1939, is printed these later papers would probably be included. My contributions to the subject are written in three different languages and the four papers have appeared in four different periodicals. Although they contain what is essential they are disparate, taking up the problems from various aspects. Considering the importance of the subject I have found it more to the purpose, instead of reprinting these writings, to rework them into a coherent whole, coordinating and completing them. Large sections of these papers have been incorporated in the present book, but the work is now more inclusive, the recasting more thorough, and the additions greater than I imagined when I began the task. The materials in some way relevant to the inquiry increased, and it also proved necessary to analyze the representations at somewhat greater length. Illustrations could be added that are missing in the papers, but are much needed for understanding the discussion of the monuments. The works of art pertaining to our subject are numerous, especially the sarcophagi, and I am sorry that my age compels me to limit myself to such as are already published. Nor have I included some monuments that are pictured or discussed in the writings of other scholars on the Bacchic mysteries, namely those which are of dubious interpretation or which do not throw any light on my subject. I am content to discuss only such as really contribute to our knowledge of the Bacchic mysteries. It was impossible, however, to limit the research to those Bacchic cults that are expressly stated to be mysteries or mystic. For the same elements and symbols that appear in these are conspicuous

---

e materiali di storia delle religioni, x, 1934, pp. 1 ff., reprinted in my Opuscula Selecta, ii, 1952, pp. 524 ff.

[10] Geschichte der griechischen Religion, ii, 1950, pp. 94 ff. and 341 ff.

[11] Dionysos Liknites, Bull. de la société des lettres de Lund, 1951—52, No. 1.

[12] The Bacchic Mysteries of the Roman Age, Harvard Theological Review, xlvi, 1953, pp. 175 ff.

[13] New Evidence for the Dionysiac Mysteries, Eranos, liii, 1955, pp. 28 f.

also in the public cults and pageants. There is no sharp limit
between the two categories. One should not forget the loose use
of the words 'mysteries' and 'mystic'. This is especially apparent in Asia Minor. Whereas the old mysteries were hidden in
secrecy, the Bacchic mysteries were not. Otherwise, we should
not have so many representations that refer to their ceremonies,
even though these are mostly transferred into the mythological
sphere, as are also the representations which give some hint of
the contents of other mysteries, e. g. the Eleusinian.

II. The Hellenistic Age.

1. The orgia. In classical times the orgia of Dionysos are
well known through many descriptions in the literature and
through numerous works of art, both sculpture and vase paintings.[1] Nor were they forgotten in the Hellenistic age, when
in a milder form they were adapted to the public cult.

Plutarch relates that on one occasion the Thyiads, without
knowing it, arrived exhausted at Amphissa in the night and lay
down to sleep in the market place.[2] This is said to have happened during the second Holy War, i. e. in the middle of the
fourth century B. C. Plutarch mentions the Thyiads at Delphi
more than once. They formed a body at the head of which was
a leader, a female ἀρχηγός. In the curious rite of the Charila,
celebrated every eighth year, she took the doll representing
Charila and carried it to a place full of ravines where it was
buried.[3] In the same passage Plutarch speaks of the Herois, a
rite mentioned only here. He says that the explanation of it is

---

The old paper by A. Rapp, Die Mänade im griech. Cultus, in der Kunst
u⸱ ⸱n der Poesie, Rhein. Mus., xxvii, 1872, pp. 1 ff., is still useful, although the
⸱ ⸱ertaining to art is utterly antiquated.
Plutarch, mul. virt., p. 249 E f.
⸱ Plutarch, quaest. graecae, 12, p. 293 E.

mainly a secret story known only to the Thyiads, but that from the ritual one might guess that it refers to the bringing up of Semele. In Plutarch's time the leader of the Thyiads was his friend Klea to whom he dedicated his tract on Isis and Osiris.[4] In the same chapter he speaks of the awakening of the Liknites by the Thyiads; we return to this interesting notice below.

A group of Athenian Thyiads went to Delphi and celebrated the orgia together with the Delphic Thyiads. Pausanias says: "I could not understand why Homer spoke of the fair dancing grounds of Panopeus till it was explained to me by the women whom the Athenians call Thyiads. These Thyiads are Attic women who go every other year with the Delphian women to Parnassus and there hold orgies in honour of Dionysos. It is the custom of these Thyiads to dance at various places on the road from Athens, and one of these places is Panopeus".[5] Evidently the Athenian Thyiads were a body of women who joined the Delphic Thyiads to celebrate the orgia in the classical place, Mt. Parnassus. The orgia were limited to certain groups of women; not everybody who wished was admitted.

The passages quoted from Plutarch are a century and a half later than the end of the Hellenistic age, but they are adduced to show that the old orgia survived throughout that period. On the other hand it appears that in Plutarch's time the Thyiads were influenced by the syncretism of the age; his friend Klea, to whom he dedicated his tract on Isis and Osiris, ·which is itself full of syncretistic speculations, had also been initiated into the mysteries of Isis. But this is another story.

The orgia were celebrated at some places in Asia Minor in the Hellenistic age. A long inscription speaks of their introduction at Magnesia ad M.[6] A portent had occurred. An image of

---

[4] Plutarch, de Iside etc., p. 364 E, ἀρχικλὰ μὲν οὖσαν ἐν Δελφοῖς τῶν Θυιάδων.

[5] Pausanias, x, 4, 3; Frazer's translation.

[6] I. Magn., 215; Quandt pp. 162 ff. It was engraved on altar by Apollonios Mokolles in the reign of Hadrian, copied from an old inscription. The original may be a forgery in connection with the demand of the city for asylia in 221/0 B. C. (Pomtow, Jahrb. f. class. Philologie, cliii, 1896, p. 755), but even if so it is of importance, for a forgery must be adapted to the circumstances

Dionysos had been found in a plane tree split open by a storm. The people applied to the Delphic oracle for advice. The god advised them to build a temple and appoint a priest for Dionysos, and to fetch Maenads of the house of Ino from Thebes to establish orgia and noble customs (νόμιμα ἐσθλά) and found Bacchic thiasi in the city. According to the oracle three Maenads were sent from Thebes· Kosko organized the thiasus of the Platanistai, Baubo that before the city (πρὸ πολεως), and Thettale that of the Kataibatai. When they died they were buried by the Magnesians in certain places.

A tomb inscription from Miletus on a priestess of late Hellenistic age[7] shows that orgia of which she was the leader were celebrated there. The townswomen are asked to bid farewell to the priestess, who had "led them to the mountain and brought all orgia and sacred things for the sake of the whole city". Still more important is a cult regulation from the same city dated in 276/5 B. C.,[8] part of a document concerning the sale of the priesthood of Dionysos. It begins with the ordinance that when the priestess (performs) sacrifice on behalf of the city it is for-

---

of the time in which it is fabricated. It is significant for *his* time that Apollonios calls himself an ἀρχαῖος μύστης.

[7] Wiegand, 4. Bericht u. s. w., Sitz-ber. Akad. Berlin, 1905, p. 547; Haussoullier, Bacchantes milésiennes, Rev. ét. grecques, xxxii, 1919, p. 256; Peek, 1344.   τὴν στήλην χαίρειμ πολιήτιδες εἴπατε Βάκχαι,
            ἱρείην· χρηστῆ τοῦτο γυναικὶ θέμις.
        ὑμᾶς εἰς ὄρος ἦγε καὶ ὄργια πάντα καὶ ἱρὰ
            ἤνεικεμ πάσης ἐρχομένη πρὸ πόλεως.
        τοὔνομα δ' εἴ τις ξεῖνος ἀνείρηται· Ἀλκμειῶνος
            Ἡροδίου καλῶν ιοῖραν ἐπισταμένη.

[8] Quandt, p. 171., LSAM, 48, with a complete bibliography, ὅταν δὲ ἡ ἱέρεια ἐπι . . . . . ηι τὰ ἱερὰ ὑπὲρ τῆς πόλ[εω]ς . . . . μὴ ἐξεῖναι ὠμοφάγιον ἐμβαλεῖν μηθενὶ πρότερον [ἢ ἡ ἱέ]ρεια ὑπὲρ τῆς πόλεως ἐμβάληι, μὴ ἐξεῖναι δὲ μηδὲ [συν-] αγαγεῖν τὸν θίασον μηθενὶ πρότερον τοῦ δημοσίου· [ἐὰ]ν δέ τις ἀνὴρ ἢ γυνὴ βούληται θύειν τῶι Διονύσωι, [πρ]οιεράσθω ὁπότερον ἂν βούληται ὁ θύων καὶ λαμβανέτω τὰ γέρη ὁ προιερώμενος. 13, δὲ τὴν ἱέρειαν γυναῖκας διδόναι Δ-INA . . . . . [τ]ὰ δὲ τέλεστρα <καὶ τελεστ> παρέχ[ειν ταῖς γυναιξὶν] ἐν τοῖς ὀργί[οις πᾶ]σιν · ἐὰν δέ τις θύειν βούλ[ηται τῶ]ι Διονύσωι γυνή, διδότω γέρη τῆι ἱερείαι σπλάγχνα, νεφ[ρόν], σκολιόν, ἱερὰμ μοῖραν, γλῶσσαν, σκέλος εἰς κοτυληδόνα [ἐκτ]ετμημένον· καὶ ἐάν τις γυνὴ βούληται τελεῖν τῶι Διονύσωι τῶι Βακχίωι ἐν τῆι πόλει ἢ ἐν τῆι χώραι ἢ ἐν ταῖς νήσοις, [ἀπο]διδότω τῆι ἱερείαι στατῆρα κατ' ἑκάστην τριετηρίδα.

bidden for anyone to 'lay down' an omophagion before the priestess has laid one down on behalf of the city, or for anyone to gather a thiasus before the public one has been gathered. The following lines concern financial matters. Lines 14 f. prescribe that the priestess shall supply the things needed for initiation.[9] Finally it is ordained, lines 18 ff., that if any woman wishes to perform initiations to Dionysos Bacchios she must pay a stater to the priestess every trieteris. This inscription provides a most curious example of regulating the old, savage orgia. The raw meal has dwindled and become a mere portion of raw flesh, laid down somewhere, and probably understood as an offering. The priestess who is the leader of the orgia buys her priesthood from the city and receives certain dues from those who sacrifice or are initiated. Though other women are permitted to form thiasi, they must pay a fee to the priestess, and the public thiasus has precedence. One may imagine how the Dionysiac ecstasy fared under such civic regulations. Not all may have been content.

In other places the orgia may have been celebrated more freely according to old custom. Diodorus Siculus[10] says that in many Greek cities the women assemble to celebrate Bacchic festivals every other year, and that it is customary for the maidens to carry thyrsi and join in the frenzied revels with shouts of Evoe, while the matrons sacrifice to the god and celebrate the Bacchic festivals in groups. Probably this pertains to his own age and is not simply borrowed from the literature.

The latest of the Alexandrian epigrammatists, Dioscorides, has

---

[9] Liddell and Scott translate τέλεστρα 'fees for admission to priesthood', referring to IG, xii:7, 237 line 27 = SIG, 1047, line 17 from Amorgos. This is impossible, the word signifies 'things needed for the initiation'. This is the sense of the word in the Milesian inscription and is clear in that from Amorgos, an ordinance concerning the priesthood of the Great Mother, where lines 26 ff. fix the dues when the priestess undertakes an initiation, part going to the priestess: then follows: ἡ δὲ αἱρουμέν[η ἀ]εὶ ἱέρεια παρεχέ[τω αὐ] τῇ τὰ τέλεστρα ἰδίαι.

[10] Diodorus Sic., iv, 3, Διὸ καὶ παρὰ πολλαῖς τῶν Ἑλληνίδων πόλεων διὰ τριῶν ἐτῶν βακχεῖά τε γυναικῶν ἀθροίζεσθαι καὶ ταῖς παρθένοις νόμιμον εἶναι θυρσοφορεῖν καὶ συνενθουσιάζειν εὐαζούσαις καὶ τιμώσαις τὸν θεόν· τὰς δὲ γυναῖκας κατὰ συστήματα θυσιάζειν τῷ θεῷ καὶ βακχεύειν καὶ καθόλου τὴν παρουσίαν ὑμνεῖν τοῦ Διονύσου μιμουμένας τὰς ἱστορουμένας τὸ παλαιὸν παρεδρεύειν τῷ θεῷ μαινάδας.

written a tomb epigram on the orgiophantes Aleximenes.[11] The scene is laid at Amphipolis on the Strymon, and the usual Bacchic revel is described, — — the tympanon, the Thyiads dancing with flying locks. But here the leader of the orgia is a man, Aleximenes. The writer may have used literary clichés but he cannot have made the orgiophantes a man, if at his time there were not Bacchic mysteries, similar to the orgia, in which men as well as women took part. This may represent a transitional stage between the old orgia, which were celebrated by women exclusively,[12] and the new Dionysiac mysteries that were open to men as well as to women.

2. *Asia Minor and the Islands.* Several inscriptions from the islands of the Aegean and Asia Minor speak of mystic Bacchic cults.[13] The sources are brief and give no information concerning the rites; sometimes it may even be doubted if the cult really comprised mysteries. In certain cases the mystic cult is affiliated to an old cult, and we shall find further instances of this in the Roman age. The Hellenistic age was fond of mysteries and may have enlarged an old cult by adding them, while still preserving elements of the old cult. This may be the cause of the lack of uniformity that we find in the Dionysiac mysteries.

A sorely mutilated inscription from Methymna on Lesbos contains prescriptions for a pannychis; the word θύρσος in the last line proves that it was Bacchic; it was celebrated by women, men being excluded except for the γυναικονόμος[14] who, of

---

[11] Anthol. pal., vii, 485, εἰς Ἀλεξιμένην ὀργιοφάντην.

βάλλεθ' ὑπὲρ τύμβου πολιὰ κρίνα καὶ τὰ συνήθη
τύμπαν' ἐπὶ στήλῃ ῥήσσετ' Ἀλεξιμένους
καὶ περιδινήσασθε μακρῆς ἀνελίγματα χαίτης
Στρυμονίην ἄφετοι Θυιάδες ἀμφὶ πόλιν
ἣ γλυκερὰ πνεύσαντος ἐφ' ὑμετέροισιν + αδαπταισ
πολλάκι πρὸς μαλακοὺς τοῦσδ' ἐχόρευε νόμους.

[12] The Lydian stranger who leads the Maenads in Euripides' Bacchae, vv. 233 ff., is Dionysos himself.

[13] Cp. the chapter, de Bacchi mysteriis culto, in Quandt, pp. 241 ff.

[14] LS, 121; IG, xii:2, 499. The supplement [γυναι]κονόμος is mine, Griech. Feste, p. 282 n. 4; so also Ziehen in LS.

course, had to see to it that no disorder arose. A sacrificial calendar from Erythrae mentions a pannychis for Dionysos Phleus.[15] On Rhodes trieteric Baccheia were celebrated by an association.[16] On Thera an association of Bacchists honour an official of the Ptolemaic king, and admit him, his wife, and his descendants as members of their thiasus.[17] An inscription from Cos of late Hellenistic times gives rules for the sale of the priesthood of Dionysos Thyllophoros and for the initiation of his priestess.[18] The cult had a mystic aspect, for it is prescribed that no woman except the priestess is permitted to sacrifice or to perform initiations to Dionysos Thyllophoros.

At Cnidus a decree of the people, to whom the Bacchi had referred the matter, forbade anyone to take up quarters in the sanctuary of Dionysos Bacchos in order that it might be kept pure.[19] However, it is not certain that this cult was mystic. This is evident, however, in a dedication to Διονύσῳ ἀρχεβάκχῳ καὶ τοῖς μύσταις from Seleucia on Kalykadnos.[20] At Cyme a stele with a honorary decree was set up in the Baccheion and is said to be sacred to τῷ Διονύσῳ τῶν θιασωτᾶν τῶμ Μενεκλείδα.[21] The Bacchic thiasus is here assembled around and named after a certain man who was its head, as in so many other Hellenistic associations.

Dionysos was one of the foremost gods of Pergamon. Not only was he the god of the theatre, but the kings stood in a special relation to him: he was probably hailed as their ancestor, and the kings appointed his priest, chosen from among their

---

[15] Österr. Jahreshefte, xiii, 1910, Beiblatt, p. 34 No. 5; Quandt p. 150. The epithet is written variously: he is an old god; see my GGR, i, p. 552, 2nd ed. p. 584.

[16] IG, xii:1, 155, second century B. C., lines 49 f., ἐν τᾶι τῶν Βακχείων ὑπο-δοχᾶι κατὰ τριετηρίδα.

[17] IG, xii:3, Suppl. 129; OGI, 735. These people were foreigners, probably soldiers; the inscription is not written in the Doric dialect.

[18] SIG, 1012.

[19] SIG, 978; LSAM, 55; about 250 B. C.

[20] Heberdey und Wilhelm, Reisen in Kilikien, Denkschriften, Akad. Wien, xliv:6, 1896, p. 104 No. 183, second century B. C.

[21] Bull. corr. hell., li, 1927, p. 375, second century B. C.

own relatives.[22] Three letters, one from Attalos II and two from Attalos III, concern his cult and his priests.[23] In the second of these Attalos III informs the Cyzicenians that his uncle (Attalos II) and he himself have appointed Athenaios a priest of Dionysos Kathegemon because they held him worthy of this honour and because he would appropriately conduct the mysteries. An altar dedicated to the deified Eumenes II by the Βάχχοι τοῦ εὐαστοῦ θεοῦ [24] certainly refers to the same god. The epithet is poetic and shows an affinity to the orgiastic cult, but the members were men. These mysteries flourished in the Roman age and we must come back to them.

Of the festivals or cults mentioned in the inscriptions cited two were pannychides and to at least one of them only women were admitted. In other cases the members of the Bacchic associations were men, as is proved by the words used in the inscriptions from Pergamon and Seleucia. But on Thera the Bacchists admitted a woman to membership. In the Hellenistic age, then, some Bacchic mysteries or mystic cults were reserved for women, others for men, and in at least one case a woman was admitted to a Bacchic association. A tendency to fuse the Bacchic cults into one, comprising both men and women, was natural, and where mystic cults were affiliated to public cults that were open to men as well as to women, this may have helped to bring together both sexes in Bacchic cults of a mystic character.

Finally we may recall the arrival of Mark Antony at Ephesus. He posed as Dionysos and the Ephesians went out to greet him accordingly:[25] the women dressed as Bacchants, the men and boys as Satyrs and Pans, and the city was full of ivy and thyrsi, harps, Pan's pipes, and flutes. This is a nice example of the fondness in Asia Minor for Bacchic pageants, of which we shall hear more.

---

[22] Referring to previous works E. Ohlemutz, Die Kulte und Götter in Pergamon, Diss. Giessen, 1940, pp. 90 ff., discusses the problems at length.

[23] I. Perg., 248; OGI, 331; Quandt, pp. 120 ff.

[24] Athen. Mitt., xxvii, 1902, p. 94 No. 86; Quandt, p. 120.

[25] Plutarch, Antonius, 24.

3. *Egypt.* The Ptolemaic kings favoured the cult of Dionysos. The gorgeous procession instituted by Ptolemy Philadelphos and described at length by Callixenus of Rhodes[26] deserves to be mentioned, for most of the paraphernalia of the cults and mysteries of Dionysos were given a place in it, even if the figures and objects shown were drawn from the common stock of imagery and descriptions found in the literature. A giant statue of Dionysos was the central figure, accompanied by a numerous train of his followers — — Satyrs, Silenus, Bacchants. His image stood in a σκιάς, a canopy of ivy and vines decorated with fruits of every kind and with wreaths, fillets, thyrsi, tympana, mitrae, and satyric, comic and tragic masks. The car on which he was carried was followed by priests and priestesses, by hierostolistai, by thiasi of every kind and by women carrying likna, Mimallones and Bassarai and Lydian women with locks flying, and wreathed, some with snakes, others with smilax, vine, and ivy. On another car stood a large image of Nyse, the nurse of Dionysos. A big thyrsus and a giant phallus followed on still other cars, besides a wine-press, wine-sacks, drinking vessels, and a Bacchic grotto from which a spring of wine and another of milk streamed forth. Dionysos was recognized as the god of wine.

The devotion of Ptolemy Philopator to Dionysos is well known, and the testimonies need not be repeated here. Of great importance to our subject is the edict in which he ordered all who performed initiations into Dionysiac mysteries throughout the land to come to Alexandria and present themselves before a certain official; there they were to give information, signed with their names, stating from whom, to the third generation, they had received the holy rites (τὰ ἱερά), and were to deliver up the holy writings (τὸν ἱερὸν λόγον), sealed and with their names.[27] The purpose of this edict has been vigorously and variously discussed. At all events it shows the king's interest in the Dionysiac mysteries. Its chief importance to us is that it

---

[26] In Athenaeus, v, p. 198 C ff.

[27] References in my GGR, ii, p. 153 n. 2; add F. Sokolowski, Encore sur le décret de Ptolomée Philopator, Journal of Juristic Papyrology, Warsaw, iii, 1943, pp. 139 ff. His opinion, that the edict was occasioned by fiscal interests, perhaps to sell licenses, is unconvincing.

shows that Dionysiac mysteries were widespread in Egypt in the third century B. C. Unhappily we have not the least information about their content. Orphism was known in Egypt, not only by the Alexandrian scholars who listed the titles of Orphic writings, but also by the people. A sorely mutilated papyrus refers to Orphic myths and rites as well as to Demeter and other Greek goddesses.[28] It is syncretistic. The word τελετή is read in the third line, but it is unsafe to take this word as proof that the text, which is partly in hexameters, is a mystery liturgy.

Our knowledge of the Dionysiac mysteries in Egypt in the Hellenistic age is regrettably incomplete, but what is left proves that they were of great importance to the Greeks in this country.

4. Italy. So it was also in Italy. In Magna Graecia the Dionysiac religion had old roots, was very popular, and had taken a special turn, Dionysos being combined with Demeter and Kore in their aspect of chthonic deities. This trinity was introduced into Rome in 496 B. C. and renamed Ceres, Liber, Libera. That the belief in the Underworld was especially strong is proved by the Apulian tomb vases, belonging to the end of the fourth and the beginning of the third century B. C.[29] That Orpheus is present on almost all of them shows that Orphic doctrines or myths were known. Some authors of Orphic writings are said to be from Magna Graecia or Sicily. Orphism had a home in these countries and Orphism is closely related to the Dionysiac religion. A precious testimony to Bacchic initiations and their connection with the belief in the Underworld is an oft-quoted inscription from Cumae, forbidding those who have not been initiated to Bacchus to be buried in a certain place.[30] (Fig. 1).

Not a few references in the comedies of Plautus show that Bacchants and Bacchanalia were well known to the Roman public in the beginning of the second century B. C. Since

---

[28] Kern, Orphic. fragm., 31; see my GGR, ii, p. 232 with n. 2.

[29] Brief survey in my GGR, i, pp. 776 f., second ed. pp. 824 f.

[30] Notizie degli scavi, 1905, p. 378; Cumont, Les religions orientales dans le paganisme romain, 4th ed., p. 197, fig. 12. οὐ θέμις ἐντοῦθα κεῖσθαι (ε)ὶ μὲ τὸν βεβαχχευμένον. Early fifth century B. C.

Fig. 1. *Inscription from Cumae.*

Plautus died probably in 186 B. C. the references are on the whole earlier than the repression of the Bacchanalia, which occurred in that year.[31] In the Aulularia the cook Congrio, who has been thrashed by the old man, complains, v. 408, that he has never before come to cook for Bacchants in a Bacchanal, and when the old man appears he exclaims: "the Bacchanal begins, he is here": the Bacchanalia are compared with a sound thrashing. The young man whom the two sisters try to seduce replies, Bacchides, v. 53: "I fear you, Bacchis, and your Bacchanal", and the slave says of them, v. 371: "the Bacchides are not Bacchides but the wildest of Bacchants, they suck the blood of a man". In the Amphitruo Alcmene's husband arrives home the morning after the night in which Jupiter has visited her in the guise of Amphitruo. In consequence a bad misunderstanding arises between him and his wife and an altercation ensues. The slave sums up the situation, v. 703: "if you oppose a Bacchant who is seized by the Bacchic frenzy *(Bacchae bacchanti)*, you make her still more insane than she is and she will hit you all the more". Very important is a verse in the Miles gloriosus, 1016,

---

[31] Casina, vv. 978 ff., the old man who presents himself with torn clothes lays the blame on the Bacchants, but is told that Bacchants do not revel now; he is forced to acknowledge this. This has been referred to the repression of the Bacchanalia: see A. Bruhl, Liber Pater, pp. 112 f., but the suggestion is not convincing.

where Milphidippida who is busy with an intrigue says to the slave Palaestrio: *"cedo signum, si harunc Baccharum es"* (give the password if you are one these Bacchants). He replies: "a certain woman loves a certain man". This proves that the Bacchants had secret organizations and signs by which they recognized each other, and that men as well as women took part in these organizations. So it was also in other mysteries of a later age, in which the password often was a sacred formula.

We cannot know how much in these passages Plautus took over from the Greek comedies that he translated and reworked, and how much he has added on his own. But it is clear that he would not have used such expressions if his audience did not understand them. They show that the festivals of the Bacchants were looked at askance, that people thought that the Bacchants were insane and their conduct violent. This picture of the Bacchants and the mention of their organization belong to the time just before the scandalous affair of the Bacchanalia in 186 B. C. and fill in the background for it.

Our sources for this famous affair are two: the Senatus Consultum de Bacchanalibus of 186 B. C. and the long account in Livy. Both are regrettably deficient in certain respects. The Senatus Consultum gives no information about the rites, while Livy's account is influenced by the traditional picture of the Bacchic orgia and cannot be trusted for the details.[32] The narrative of Livy consists of two different parts. One is the brief account of the eighth chapter, according to which an ignoble Greek from Etruria, *sacrificulus et vates, occultorum et nocturnorum antistes sacrorum*, is said to have initiated the Bacchic movement. The other, found in the following chapters, is the dramatic story of the courtesan Hispala and her lover Aebutius. Here a Campanian woman, Paculla Annia, is said to have changed the rites and initiated her sons, Minius and Herennius Cerrinius. Because of the intimate details one may suspect that this account is derived from a family tradition of the Postumii

---

[32] Livy, xxxix, 8 ff. The Senatus Consultum and the passage of Livy have been often discussed; the most recent treatment is in Bruhl, Liber Pater, pp. 82 ff., with references to earlier literature.

or the Sulpicii.[33] These two accounts need not be considered contradictory. Considering the extension of the Bacchic movement, as testified to by Plautus, it is only natural if leaders arose in various places, won adherents, and propagated and reformed the rites. This view is confirmed by the notice in ch. xvii that the leaders of the conspiracy were not only the Campanian Minius Cerrinius, but also two Roman plebeians, M. and C. Atinius, and the Faliscan L. Opicernius.

Livy's account is embellished by romantic and exaggerated details. Some are drawn from the common stock of descriptions of the revelling Bacchants; his report of their terrible crimes remind us too much of the horrors commonly ascribed to a despised and persecuted religion by their adversaries, e. g. the abominable rites imputed to the Christians or the Jews by their foes. To try and sift out the real facts underlying Livy's narrative is an impossible task, and any judgment must be to a high degree subjective. It will be better to relate the pertinent parts and let the reader himself judge according to the best of his ability.

On the Bacchanalia instituted by the ignoble Greek he says:[34] "There were initiatory rites which at first were imparted to a few, then began to be generally known among men and women. To the religious element in them were added the delights of wine and feasts, that the minds of a larger number might be attracted. When wine had inflamed their minds, and night

---

[33] There were historians in both families. Dr Hanell points to A. Postumius Albinus, praetor urbanus 155 and consul 151 B. C., who wrote a history in Greek of which only a quotation from the first book, referring to Brutus, is preserved. Polybius, xxxix, 12, 4, calls the work 'pragmatic'. Cicero says of the author that he was learned, Acad. pr., ii, 137, and *litteratus et disertus*, Brutus, 81. One may also refer to the Sulpicii, for the consul of 186 B. C., Sp. Postumius Albinus, took counsel with his mother-in-law, who was a Sulpicia, and she was present at his interview with Hispala. One Sulpicius Blitho is quoted by Cornelius Nepos, Hannibal, 13, 1, for the date of the death of Hannibal. C. Sulpicius Galba, grandfather of the emperor, wrote Rome's history to his own time. It is quoted by Plutarch, Romulus, 17, 2, and Orosius, v, 23, 6, where Pompey and Sertorius are mentioned.

[34] In ch. viii. Translations (adapted) by E. T. Sage in the Loeb Classical Library. G. Méautis, Les aspects religieux de l'affaire des Bacchanales, Rev. des ét. anciennes, lxii, 1940, pp. 476 ff.

and the mingling of males with females, youth with age, had
destroyed every sentiment of modesty, all varieties of corruption first began to be practised, since each one had at hand the
pleasure answering to that to which his nature was more inclined.
There was not one form of vice alone, the promiscuous matings
of free men and women, but perjured witnesses, forged seals and
wills and evidence, all issued from this same workshop: likewise
poisonings and murders of kindred, so that at times not even the
bodies were found for burial. Much was ventured by craft, more
by violence. This violence was concealed because amid the
howlings and the crash of drums and cymbals no cry of the
sufferers could be heard as the debauchery and murders pro-
ceeded." ᐯ

The second narration begins by telling how the step-father
of the young Aebutius, having squandered his ward's fortune,
and the boy's mother wanted to get rid of him by causing him
to be initiated into the Bacchanalia. For this an abstinence from
sexual intercourse of ten days was required. When he told this
to his mistress Hispala she was terror-stricken and implored him
to desist from the project. When asked for the reason she
replied that:

x, 5. "While she was a slave she had attended her mistress to that
shrine but as a free woman she had never visited it. She knew,
she said, that it was the factory of all sorts of corruptions; and
it was known that for two years now no one had been initiated
who had passed the age of twenty years. As each was introduced,
he became a sort of victim for the priests. They, she continued,
would lead him to a place which would ring with howls and the
song of a choir and the beating of cymbals and drums, that the
voice of the sufferer, when his virtue was violently attacked,
might not be heard. Then she begged and besought him to put
an end to this matter in any way he could and not to plunge
into a situation where all disgraceful practices would have first
to be endured and then performed."

He obeyed, but was driven from home by his mother and
stepfather, took refuge with his aunt, and on her advice turned
to the consul Postumius. He summoned Hispala and held an
inquiry in the presence of his mother-in-law Sulpicia. The

courtesan was stricken with terror and tried to evade his
questions, but at last made a full confession:
xiii, 5. "She declared that she feared greatly the wrath of the gods
whose hidden mysteries she was to reveal, but far more the
wrath of the men who would, if she informed against them,
with their own hands tear her limb from limb . . . . Then
Hispala set forth the origin of the mysteries. At first, she said,
it was a ritual for women, and it was the custom that no man
should be admitted to it. There had been three days appointed
each year on which they held initiations into the Bacchic rites
by day; it was the rule to choose the matrons in turn as priestesses. Paculla Annia, a Campanian, she said, when priestess, had
changed all this as if by advice of the gods; for she had been the
first to initiate men, her sons, Minius and Herennius Cerrinius;
she had held the rites by night and not by day, and instead of
a mere three days a year she had established five days of initiation in every month. From the time that the rites were performed in common, men mingling with women and the freedom of
darkness added, no form of crime, no sort of wrongdoing, was
left untried. There were more lustful practices among men with
one another than among women. If any of them were disinclined
to endure abuse or reluctant to commit crime, they were sacrificed as victims.[35] To consider nothing wrong, she continued,
was the highest form of religious devotion among them. Men, as
if insane, with fanatical tossings of their bodies, would utter
prophecies. Matrons in the dress of Bacchants, with dishevelled
hair and carrying blazing torches, would run down to the Tiber,
and plunging their torches in the water (because they contained
live sulphur mixed with calcium) would bring them out still
burning. Men were alleged to have been carried off by the gods
who had been bound to a machine and borne away out of sight
to hidden caves:[36] they were those who had refused either to

---

[35] Cumont, Les religions orientales etc., 4th ed., p. 198, thinks it probable
that the rites performed recalled the murder of the child Dionysos by the
Titans and that possibly at times the Bacchants in their sacred ravings may have
torn a human victim to pieces. I am not persuaded.

[36] It is not likely that such a machine was used in the grove of Stimula (ms
in luco Similae Bacchanalibus in sacro nocturno, Livy, xxxix, 12, 5; some scholars

conspire or to join in the crimes or to suffer abuse. Their number, she said, was very great, almost constituting a second state;
among them were certain men and women of high rank. Within
the last two years it had been ordained that no one beyond the
age of twenty years should be initiated: persons of such age
were sought for as admitted both vice and corruption."

An extraordinary session of the senate was convoked and
strict measures taken to prevent the guilty from escaping, and
to confine them. Then the consul called an assembly of the
people and delivered a speech which Livy relates in ch. xv. A
few lines of this may be quoted:

xv, 6. "As to the Bacchanalia, I am assured that you have learned
that they have long been celebrated all over Italy and now even
within the city in many places, and that you have learned this
not only from rumour but also from their din and cries at night,
which echo throughout the city, but I feel sure that you do not
know what this thing is: some believe that it is a form of worship
of the gods, others that it is an allowable play and pastime, and,
whatever it is, that it concerns only a few."

Livy ends ch. xvii by saying that there was great fear in the
city, which spread throughout the whole of Italy. Many who
tried to fly were seized, many were denounced, some committed
suicide. It was said that seven thousand men and women had
conspired. More people suffered capital punishment than were
imprisoned. It is, however, a little surprising that Minius Cerrinius, one of the chief personages, was spared and confined at
Ardea; the officials at Ardea were enjoined to see not only that
he did not escape but also that he did not commit suicide.

The Senatus Consultum de Bacchanalibus[37] is quoted in Livy
in such words that it appears likely that he (or better the author
whom he used) was familiar with the document itself. It forbids
the Bacchanalia, and it forbids the performance of secret rites in
public or private places, or outside the city. But an exception is
conceded because of religious scruples: if some persons say that
it is necessary for them to celebrate the Bacchanalia, they must

---

correct: *Semelae)* near the Aventine and the Tiber. The description calls to
mind the machines used on the stage to carry away persons or to let gods appear.

[37] CIL, i, 2nd ed., 581; ILS, i, 18 etc., Livy, xxxix, 18, 7 f.

bring the matter before the praetor urbanus in Rome, who in turn refers it to the senate. The senate, provided there is a quorum of at least a hundred senators present, may grant permission, but otherwise all persons are forbidden to visit the Bacchants. But even this permission is safeguarded by severe restrictions. A man is not permitted to be a priest (the priesthood is evidently reserved for a woman); no one, either man or woman, is permitted to be a *magister*, viz. leader of a group. It is not permitted to have a common treasure or any officials (*magistratus, promagistratus*). In very explicit words the Bacchants are forbidden to give one another promises, vows of fidelity, or oaths of allegiance. Not more than five persons, two men and three women, are allowed to perform sacrifices (or rites, *sacra*), except with the approval, obtained as above of the praetor urbanus and the senate.

It is evident that the senate considered the Bacchic associations a genuine threat to the public security, and the consul Postumius stated this in so many words in his speech to the people as related by Livy. That is why the organization of the associations was crushed, why they were not allowed to have officials or money. But religious scruples prevented forbidding the Bacchanalia completely, nor was it possible to forbid the cult of Bacchus in general since he was an acknowledged member of the pantheon; even so it seems that the public cult too was subjected to some restriction. After lines 15 ff., which forbid secret cults, follows the paragraph (lines 19 ff.) prescribing that no more than two men and three women may regularly be present at a sacrifice. This restriction seems to be added in order that the Bacchanalia might not be perpetuated under cover of a public cult.

The public cult of Bacchus must necessarily be continued. A temple said to be dedicated to Bacchus and Ariadne, discovered in 1947 on the hill of S. Abbondio near Pompeii, seems to be roughly contemporaneous with the incidents here described. The altar before the temple has an inscription in the Oscan dialect with the name of the *aedilis, Maras Atiniis*.[38] It is a

---

[38] I know it only through a notice in Bruhl, Liber Pater, p. 86.

remarkable coincidence that the two Roman plebeians who
were involved in the affair had the same name, but they need
not be related to the Pompeian aedile.

The trouble, however, was not ended by these drastic measures. It persisted in Southern Italy, where the Bacchic movement
had old roots and was apparently strongest. Moreover, the land
was devastated and misery was great, only twenty years having
elapsed since Hannibal's departure. In 184 B. C. the praetor L.
Postumius, governor of Tarentum, put down a great conspiracy
of herdsmen and carried out conscientiously the measures
against the Bacchanalia.[39] He himself passed sentence on many
guilty persons who had concealed themselves in this part of
Italy, and sent others to Rome where they were put into prison.
In 181 B. C. the praetor L. Duronius, governor of Apulia, had
still to busy himself with the Bacchanalia, of which vestiges had
appeared again in the foregoing year. The senate ordered him to
quell the movement.[40]

The energetic and merciless action of the Senate did at last
repress the Bacchanalia, and in the following years nothing is
heard of them. A small remnant, however, was left, and the
public cult of Bacchus continued. It can surely be assumed that
the Bacchic movement lived underground. For in the last years
of the Republic new Bacchic mysteries became popular. It is
said that Caesar introduced the Bacchic mysteries into Rome.[41]
This is not true, but may imply that he, like Antony, favoured
them: he was not attached to the old Roman traditions. But
these new mysteries were very dissimilar to the Bacchanalia.
Those had been akin to the Greek orgia in their ecstatic fanaticism, and were celebrated outdoors in secret places. The new
mysteries were free from fanaticism, and they were probably

---

[39] Livy, xxxix, 41, 6 f. The Latin word is *pastores*. It has been supposed that
this is a translation of the Greek word βουκόλοι, used ,to denote members of
the Bacchic associations. But is must also be remembered that as a consequence
of political measures there were large areas of pasture grounds in Southern Italy
and many herdsmen.

[40] Livy, xl, 19, 9.

[41] Servius ad Verg., Ecl., v, 29, *Caesarem constat primum sacra Liberi patris
Romam transtulisse.*

celebrated indoors, at least in certain cases. They had new symbols. Although Hispala says that certain noblemen and gentlewomen were found in the Bacchanalia, it is certain that the adherents chiefly belonged to the lower classes, plebeians or people in Italy who were not Roman citizens; the chief seat was Southern Italy. The monuments prove that the new Bacchic mysteries at the end of the Republic were favoured, on the contrary, by rich and wealthy people.

It is difficult to say where this profound change originated and from what point it came to Italy. It may be guessed that it was from Asia Minor or Egypt, and that these impulses were fused with beliefs and practices at home in old Magna Graecia. We shall come back to the Bacchic mysteries in Italy of the last years of the Republic and the following centuries in our sixth chapter.

III. The Liknon.

The liknon filled with fruit among which a phallus rises, often covered with a cloth, is the characteristic symbol of the Bacchic mysteries of the Roman age, and the god named after it, Dionysos Liknites, is often mentioned in modern writings on the Dionysiac religion. Before we enter upon these mysteries an inquiry into the origin of the liknon as a religious symbol and into the significance of Dionysos Liknites is needed.

The liknon is defined by the lexicographers as a sieve or winnowing shovel.[1] It was an oblong basket of wickerwork of a special shape. One of the small ends is open, the sides rise gradually towards the other end, which is closed, and on each side is a handle. It was an agricultural implement. After the sheaves had been threshed on the threshing floor the corn mixed with chaff was laid in the liknon, and by shaking it the corn was

---

[1] Suidas, Photius, Λίχνον· κόσκινον ἤτοι πτύον.

separated from the chaff.[2] The procedure is described graphically in Homer:[3]

> When in the holy threshing floors away the wind doth bear
> the chaff, when men are winnowing, She of the golden hair
> Demeter with the rushing winds the husk from out the grain
> divideth, and the chaff-heaps whiten and grow amain.

For its special purpose the liknon was needed for only a few days at harvest time, but it could be, and was, used like other baskets for other purposes, for a Greek household had no abundance of vessels and implements. The liknon was at hand and was practical for carrying certain objects, including a baby. It was appropriate for this, having handles on both sides just like a modern baby-basket, and that it was so used is explicitly stated by ancient authors.[4] The sides prevented the baby from rolling out and it could not leap up. Of course Hermes did, but he was a god and that was a miracle.[5]

In order to clear up the origin of the liknon as a sacred symbol we must begin with its sacral use in times before the Hellenistic age. We must keep clearly in mind a distinction of decisive importance. Any implement can occasionally be employed in sacral use, e. g. at a sacrifice or in a procession offerings or sacred utensils are carried in an ordinary basket. It is not sacred in itself. On the other hand certain implements and certain symbols are sacred, e. g. an altar, or the thyrsus. Not much is

---

[2] On various implements, both ancient and modern, used for the same purpose see the fundamental paper by J. E. Harrison, Mystica vannus Iacchi, Journ. of Hellenic Studies, xxiii, 1903, pp. 292 ff.; additions ibid. xxiv, 1904, pp. 241 ff., and Annual of the British School at Athens, x, 1903—04, pp. 144 ff.

[3] Translation by Jane E. Harrison. Iliad, v, 499 ff.

ὡς δ' ἄνεμος ἄχνας φορέει ἱερὰς κατ' ἀλωὰς
ἀνδρῶν λικμώντων, ὅτε τε ξανθὴ Δημήτηρ
κρίνῃ ἐπειγομένων ἀνέμων καρπόν τε καὶ ἄχνας

[4] Callimachus, Hymns, i, 47 (the child Zeus) σὲ δ' ἐκοίμισεν Ἀδρήστεια λίκνῳ
ἐνὶ χρυσέῳ; Scholia ad locum, ἐν γὰρ λίκνοις τὸ παλαιὸν κατεκοίμιζον τὰ βρέφη
πλοῦτον καὶ καρποὺς οἰωνιζόμενοι· λίκνον οὖν τὸ κόσκινον ἢ τὸ κούνιον ἐν ᾧ τὰ
παιδία τιθέασι.

[5] Hymn. hom. in Merc., vv. 150 ff.

heard of the liknon in the religion of the classical age. There are two passages in the literature, neither of which is conclusive. The earliest mention is in a fragment of Sophocles.[6] "Then go out on the street, you handicraftsmen, who supplicate the fierce-eyed daughter of Zeus with standing likna and at the anvil with the heavy hammer." More important is the mention in the description by Demosthenes of the rôle of Aeschines as a helper of his mother in the cult of Sabazios, inter alia he is said to have been a leader and guide and ivy-wreathed and a liknon-bearer (λικνοφόρος) and to have been named so by the old women. In comparison with the other functions mentioned the liknon has but an insignificant place, one may perhaps ask if it was not simply a basket without any special significance, such as was carried in processions. Of course Sabazios is akin to Dionysos but his cult was foreign and despised. It is not a certain assumption that the liknon was borrowed from the cult of Dionysos.[8]

We turn to the monuments for more information. As far as I know no monument from classical or earlier times exists in which the liknon has a specific cultual meaning, such as is common in the Hellenistic and Roman ages. Miss Harrison adduced a black-figured vase representing a wedding procession.[9] (Fig. 2). Two women carry likna and a third between them an ordinary basket. There is no need to refer to the notice half a millennium later that at a wedding a boy carried a liknon and said: "I have escaped the evil and found the better".[10] Here

---

[6] Fragm. 760 Nauck, 2nd ed. βᾶτ' εἰς ὁδὸν δὴ πᾶς ὁ χειρῶναξ λεώς, οἳ τὴν Διὸς γοργῶπιν 'Εργάνην στατοῖς λίκνοισι προτρέπεσθε.

[7] Demosth., De corona, xviii, 259.

[8] The tale of Olympias, the mother of Alexander the Great, in Plutarch, Alexander, 2, is very suspect; it is embroidered with well-known clichées: ὄφεις μεγάλους χειροήθεις ἐφείλκετο τοῖς θιάσοις, οἳ πολλάκις ἐκ τοῦ κιττοῦ καὶ τῶν μυστικῶν λίκνων παραδυόμενοι καὶ περιελιττόμενοι τοῖς θύρσοις τῶν γυναικῶν καὶ τοῖς στεφάνοις ἐξέπληττον τοὺς ἄνδρας. Elsewhere there is no mention of snakes in the liknon, only in the cista mystica. And men are said to be present at the orgia!

[9] Journ. of Hell. Studies, xxiii, 1903, p. 316 with fig. 13.

[10] Ps.-Plutarch, Proverbia Alexandrina, 16. See further my Symbolisme astronomique et mystique dans certains cultes publics grecs in Hommage à J. Bidez et F. Cumont, Collection Latomus, ii, 1949, pp. 222.

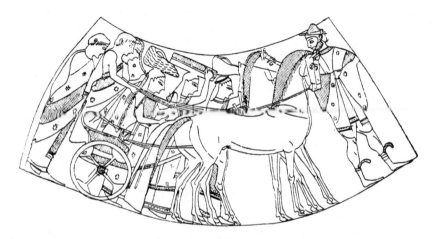

Fig. 2. *Black-figured amphora. Wedding procession.*

two women are carrying each a liknon. They are simply carrying gifts to the newly-wedded couple.

More interesting is a crater from the necropolis at Spina in the museum at Ferrara, dated about the middle of the fifth century B. C. (Fig. 3).[11] I repeat Aurigemma's description. In a temple, represented by two Doric columns, two divinities are seated. At the side of an altar before them is a priestess carrying a liknon on her head, behind her a woman playing the flute and another with cymbals, a flute-player in a richly embroidered dress, another woman with cymbals and one with a tympanon, dancing ecstatically, and women, youths, and young girls, handling snakes and with snakes in their hair. The goddess has a lion standing on her extended left arm. The vase represents a

---

[11] The vase is published by S. Aurigemma, Il r. museo di Spina, Ferrara 1953, p. 180 and pl. 96; 2nd ed. p. 210 and pl. 100. It is listed by Beazley, Attic Red-Fig. Vase-Painters, p. 696, and attributed by him to the group of Polygnotos. It is figured on a small scale in the Memoirs of the American Academy in Rome, vi, pl. 22. It is treated at length by F. Sartori, Il cratere della tomba 128 nella necropoli di Spina, Rendiconti dell'accademia dei Lincei, v, 1950, pp. 233 ff.; he has the best reproductions, pls. i—iii.

Fig. 3. *Red-figured crater from Spina. Bacchic revel.*

curious mixture of an ordinary cult and frantic orgiasm of a mythical character. This is not unparalleled, it is found e. g. on certain Anthesteria vases. Here the question concerns the liknon. It seems to be empty, its upper contour is clearly visible, and nothing is elevated above it, no erected phallus, but the sides are covered by a piece of cloth which hangs down at both the small ends. It is not the same as the liknon found on later monuments.[12]

Among the very numerous small jugs, presented to children who were admitted for the first time to the drinking festival of the Choes and profusely illustrated in the great work of Professor van Hoorn, one in the Vlasto collection in Athens is remarkable and almost exciting[13] (Fig. 4). It is earlier and much

---

[12] The identity of the gods has been much discussed. Above the head of the goddess the letters ΑΚΟΣ are seen and in front of her ΚΛΟΕ, but these inscriptions are faded and perhaps not complete. However, there does not seem to be room for an additional letter before ΚΛΟΕ. The inscriptions are repeated on the back side. Aurigemma's proposal Ἴακχος and Ἑκάτη has not been accepted. Beazley's identification with Dionysos and Ariadne does not conform to the letters. Sartori's reading: Bacchos, (Demeter) Chloe, is not acceptable, nor his interpretation, referring the representation to the Eleusinian cult, especially to the festival of the Chloia which is attested at Eleusis. But Bacchic frenzy was foreign to Eleusis and certainly also to the agrarian festival of the Chloia, of which we know nothing but what the name indicates. His attempt to account for the lion on the outstreched arm of the goddess through equating her with Artemis is not successful; the lion belongs of course to the entourage of Dionysos. K. Kérényi, ΕΚΛΟΕ, Symb. Osl., xxx, 1953, pp. 82 ff., reads the name of the god [Ἴ]αχ[χος] and that of the goddess ΕΚΛΟΕ which he takes to be Εὔκλεια, the Queen of the Underworld. The enthroned god is dissimilar to all that we otherwise hear or see of Iacchos, and he and the Queen of the Underworld would be a most disparate couple. Moreover, the linguistic equation of ΕΚΛΟΕ with Εὔκλεια is extremely doubtful. As to the liknon I do not deny that it was in sacral use in the early and classical age, but I have pointed to the fact that the liknon with fruit and a phallus does not appear as a symbol of the Bacchic mysteries until the Hellenistic age. This salient point is ignored. In an addendum, Symb. Osl., xxxi, 1955, pp. 152 f., Kérényi discusses the reading of the inscriptions. Erika Simon, Opfernde Götter, 1953, pp. 79 ff., supposes, improbably, that the divine pair is Sabazios and Kybele. That the god is Dionysos is certain, but the name of the goddess must be left unexplained.

[13] G. van Hoorn, Choes and Anthesteria, 1951, fig. 38, catalogue no. 271, p. 97; Beazley, Attic Red-Figure Vase-Painters, p. 275, 10; my GGR, i, second ed., pl. 38, 1.

Fig. 4. *Small Choes-jug. Mask of Dionysos.*

better than the great mass of these, in general, carelessly painted
small jugs and is attributed to the Eretria painter c. 430—425
B.C. In the middle is a small three-legged table, on this a liknon,
decorated with ivy sprays; from its open end a piece of cloth
hangs down, and in the liknon lies the bearded mask of Dionysos with a diadem from which ivy leaves rise. To the right is a
woman bringing some offerings on a plate or tray, to the left
another woman offering a kantharos; she brings wine which she
has drawn from a mixing vessel, placed on a low stand behind
her.

I agree wholly with Professor van Hoorn's suggestion that
the same mask which is placed in the liknon (after the resurrection of the god, he says: on this see below p. 30) was used for
the next ritual,[14] viz. the erection of a wooden pole wrapped
round with a cloth, on which the mask was hung up. The mask
was a usual prerequisite in the cult of Dionysos in the late
archaic age. It was sometimes made of marble; one such wonderful archaic marble mask was found in the village especially
devoted to the cult of Dionysos, Icaria. Masks of Dionysos or
Silenus are figured on some black-figured vases.[15] The pole with
the mask is seen on a series of vases which Frickenhaus has
collected and published under the name of *Lenäenvasen*.[16] They

[14] van Hoorn, loc. cit. p. 24; in his paper, 'La resurrection de Dionysos Liknites', Bulletin van de Vereiniging tot Bevordering der Kennis van de antieke
Beschaving te 'S-Gravenhage, xxiv—xxvi, 1949—51, pp. 7. It is to regretted
that in his reproduction of the Vlasto chous, fig. 4, the left part with the crater
has been cut away for typographical reasons; it is of importance for the interpretation of the scene.

[15] W. Wrede, 'Der Maskengott', Athen. Mitt., liii, 1928, pp. 66. E. Coche
de La Ferté, 'Les ménades et le contenu réel des representations de scènes bacchiques autour de l'idole de Dionysos', Rev. archéol., xxxviii, 1951, pp. 12.

[16] In the 72. Winckelmannsprogramm der archäologischen Gesellschaft in
Berlin, 1912. C. Q. Giglioli, 'Una nuova rappresentazione del culto attico di
Dioniso,' Annuario scuola archeol. di Atene, iv—v, 1921—22 (printed in 1924),
pp. 130, publishes fragments of a crater in Naples, dated about 490 B.C. The
scene is similar to that in Frickenhaus, pl. ii, no. 14. He discusses these vases,
reproducing many of them, e.g. the lekythos in the Czartoryski collection at
Cracow, which was not figured, only described by Frickenhaus, p. 36, no. 15.
Philippart, Rev. archéol., i, 1933, pp. 160, describes a stamnos in the collection
in the Castello Sforzesco in Milan which, owing to its bad preservation, it was

represent an idol of Dionysos consisting of a pole on which a mask is hung and around which a cloth is wrapped; before the idol women are manipulating wine vessels and sometimes dancing. The elements of the scenes depicted on the Vlasto chous and on the Anthesteria vases are the same. On the former a woman brings offerings, probably fruit and cakes, in a basket, on the latter such offerings are placed on the table before the mask idol,[17] sometimes a woman carries a basket, but of the three-horned shape, so to call it, which occurs in sacrificial scenes.[18] The great mixing vessels are there too.[19] The women offer a cup of wine to the mask idol and this is crowned and the idol surrounded with ivy sprays.[20] The difference is that on the Vlasto chous the mask is placed in a liknon, on the Anthesteria vases it is hung up on a pole. The Vlasto vase represents a preliminary act, the bringing of the mask which is to be hung up on the pole. It is a chous. Nobody will suppose, I think, that a rite of the Lenaea is depicted on a vase made expressly for the Choes. The relation of the vases which Frickenhaus and Deubner styled *Lenäenvasen* to the rites of the second day of the Anthesteria, the Choes, is demonstrated.[21]

---

not possible to photograph. The scene is identical with that of a stamnos in the British Museum, Frickenhaus, pp. 8 and 9, fig. 18 A and B. Coche de La Ferté, loc. cit., p. 12, n. 3, mentions a carelessly painted, late black-figured lekythos from Chaeronea. I have not been able to control the reference: Fragment of a stamnos in the Villa Giulia. M. Firenze, CV (1), pl. 14, 222; Beazley, Campana fragments, pl. 14,6.

[17] Frickenhaus, loc. cit., pl. iii, nos. 16 and 17, pl. v, nos. 26 and 27.

[18] Ibid., pl. v, nos. 26 and 27; on this form of the basket see Deubner, 'Hochzeit und Opferkorb', Arch. Jahrb., xl, 1925, pp. 210.

[19] Ibid., pl. ii, no. 12; iii, nos. 16 and 17.

[20] Ibid., pl. ii, no. 13; pl. iii, nos. 16 and 17; pl. v, nos. 26 and 27.

[21] L. Deubner, Attische Feste, pp. 127; my papers: 'Eine Anthesterienvase in München', Sitz.-ber. d. bayr. Akad. d. Wiss., 1930, No. 4, and 'Eine neue schwarz-figurige Anthesterienvase', Bull. de la Soc. des lettres de Lund, 1933, No. 3, both reprinted in my Opuscula selecta, i, pp. 414 and ii, pp. 457 resp.; polemizing against the latter paper, Deubner, 'Eine neue Lenäenvase', Arch. Jahrb., xlix, 1934, pp. 1. In his cited book, p. 94, he tries to evade the relation of these vases to the Choes by suggesting that the wine was brought and mixed for the god on the day of the Pithoigia, the 11th Anthesterion. In his eagerness he forgot the fact that the sanctuary in the Marshes was closed on that day, although in

I agree with Professor van Hoorn that the representation of
the Vlasto chous cannot be related to the awakening of the Liknites by the Thyiads at Delphi, to which I come back below, pp.
38 ff., but I am unable to agree with his opinion that the wine and
fruit offered by the women will serve to refresh the awakened
god, or with his final point, that in order to ennoble the primi-
tive ceremony of erecting the phallus in the liknon this crude
symbol was replaced by the noble head of the god.[22] For the
liknon with the phallus appears only in the Hellenistic age. Here
the liknon is simply used to bring the mask that is to be hung
up on the pole.

The examination of the literature and the vase paintings
shows that in the classical age the liknon was not sacred in
itself but like other profane implements sometimes occurred in
sacral use.

In the Hellenistic age we hear of the liknon in the cult of
Dionysos. It is natural that women carrying likna appear in the
procession described by Callimachus in his hymn to Demeter,
v. 126, but it is a little surprising that the likna are said to be
full of gold. Polemon, who was a good scholar living in the
beginning of the second century B.C., spoke in his treatise on
the Διὸς κώδιον of some initiation.[23] Unhappily the compiler
has left out the beginning of the quotation so that it is not
known to which cult it refers. He mentions the kernos, describes
its contents and ends: "The man who carries this (the kernos),

the following pages he quotes the testimonies which state that it was open only
one day of the year, namely the 12th Anthesterion, the day of the Choes. For
whatever the significance be of the dative πρὸς τῷ ἱερῷ in the passage of Philo-
demos, which he discusses at length, pp. 127, it cannot be said that the people
mixed the wine before the god (τῷ θεῷ κιρνάναι) if they stayed outside the
closed sanctuary. Moreover his suggestion implies a doublet of the drinking feast
of the Choes. That is unlikely. Dionysos himself was called Χοοπότης when
Themistocles instituted the festival of the Choes at Magnesia, Possis in Athenaeus,
xii, p. 533 D.

[22] van Hoorn, Choes and Anthesteria, p. 24; in his paper, quoted p. 28, n. 14,
p. 10 resp.

[23] Athen., xi, p. 478 C; A. Tresp, 'Die Fragmente der griech. Kultschriftsteller', Religionswiss. Versuche und Vorarbeiten, xv: 1, pp. 87, with parallel
passages.

just as one who carries the liknon, tastes of them".[24] It is not clear what this comparison implies, perhaps only that the man carried the liknon on his head just as another carried the kernos, perhaps some sacral rite occurring in both cases. Likna were carried in the gorgeous procession instituted by Ptolemy Philadelphos.[25] In an epigram by the Alexandrian poet Phalaikos, who lived in the time of Ptolemy Philadelphos, Euanthe dedicates to Bacchos a liknon together with the entire apparatus of a Maenad: the rousing bull-roarer, the fawnskin, the tympana, the thyrsus, the cymbals, and the liknon carried on the head.[26] Everything, except the liknon, is old and well known from the orgia.

These passages taken from the literature prove only that the liknon was used in the cult of Dionysos. They do not tell anything of its contents or significance. For this problem we must turn to the monuments.

Half a century ago Miss Harrison called attention to some Hellenistic reliefs on which the liknon appears filled with fruit, among which a phallus is erected. One of the Hellenistic landscape reliefs, said to be Alexandrian, shows in the foreground a peasant going to the market and driving in front of him a cow (Fig. 5).[27] He passes a sanctuary of Dionysos; to the left a wine cup is standing on a base against which a thyrsus and two torches are leaning. To the right a tree protrudes a branch through a gate. In the middle a high baluster rises on which a liknon is placed. A bunch of grapes hangs down from it, and it seems to be filled with vine-leaves and fruit among which a phallus rises. In the upper left-hand corner is a small temple in whose door-opening a herm is seen. It is indistinct: Miss Harrison guesses it may be Hermes or Dionysos; perhaps it is Priapus.[28]

---

[24] Loc. cit., ὁ δὲ τοῦτο βαστάσας οἷον λικνοφορήσας τούτων γεύεται.

[25] Athen., v. p. 198 E; cf. above p. 11.

[26] Anthol. pal., vi, 165, v. 5, ἠδὲ φορηθὲν πολλάκι μιτροδέτου λίκνον ὕπερθε κόμης.

[27] Harrison, Prolegomena to the Study of Greek Religion, fig. 148, p. 519. Th. Schreiber, Hellenistische Reliefbilder, pl. 80 A.

[28] Cf. below p. 36.

Fig. 5. *Hellenistic relief.*

Only a fragment is left of another relief formerly in the collection of Dr Hartwig (Fig. 6).[29] A liknon is standing on the top
of a square pillar; it is covered by a cloth whose elevation shows
that a phallus is beneath it. A small winged Eros is at the side
of the pillar. A similar pillar carrying a liknon is seen on a
relief in the Museum in Vienna (Fig. 7).[30] The liknon is not
covered, a grape cluster hangs down from it, and a phallus rises
among its contents. At the side of the pillar is a wingless Eros
(or is it the child Dionysos?). A series of Bacchic attributes are

---

[29] Harrison, Note on the Mystica Vannus Iacchi, Annual of the British School
at Athens, x, 1903—04, fig. 1 p. 145.
[30] Ibid. fig. 2.

Fig. 6. *Fragment of a Hellenistic relief,*
formerly in the collection of
Dr Hartwig.

scattered around, a lyre, masks, a tympanon, a thyrsus. The
liknon filled with fruit among which a phallus rises is here one
of the many attributes characteristic of Dionysos. It appears —
and the point is important — that this liknon is not a secret
symbol reserved for the mysteries, it is exposed openly and
publicly. It is not the Mystica vannus Iacchi.

It is not difficult to understand the liknon with fruit and a
phallus in relation to the cult of Dionysos. The god himself is
not ithyphallic but his companions, the Satyrs, were, and phalli
were carried in all processions in his honour; sometimes monu-
mental phalli were erected as votive gifts.[31] Grape clusters were
an attribute of the god of wine and they may have caused other

---

[31] It is superfluous to dwell upon this well-known subject, for more details
see the paragraph: "Der Phallos im Kult des Dionysos" in my GGR, i, pp. 557 ff.,
second ed. pp. 590 ff.

Fig. 7.   *Hellenistic relief in the Museum of Vienna.*

fruits to be added. Though the tree cult is conspicuous in the
cult of Dionysos, he is not related to other fruits than the vine.[32]

However, the third monument published by Miss Harrison
gives us pause. It is a Priapus herm in the Lateran Museum,
around which a cloth is draped and which has arms (Fig. 8).[33]
In his right hand Priapus carries a liknon, partly veiled; among
the fruits a fir-cone can be recognized, and the veil rises into a
peak because of the phallus. A child, probably Dionysos himself,
stands in the right elbow of Priapus and caresses his head. The
grape in his right hand is restored.

Priapus came from northwestern Asia Minor and was very
popular in the Hellenistic age and still more the Roman age.

---

[32] The only exception is Dionysos   συκίτης   in Sparta, who is said to be
called so because he invented fig culture, Sosibius in Athen., iii, 78 C.

[33] Loc. cit. figs. 3 and 4, p. 146.

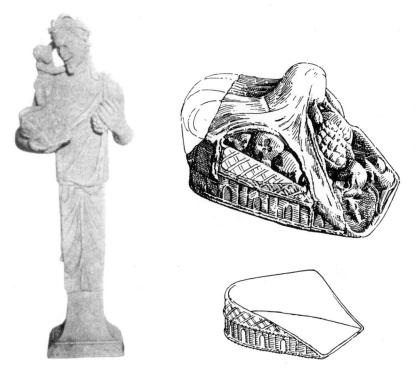

Fig. 8, a. *Priapus herm in the Lateran Museum,*
b. *Design of his liknon,* c. *A liknon.*

One need only read Horace[34] or the lascivious Carmina Priapea.
He was the guardian of gardens and their fruits, and his image
was commonly set up in gardens. Many statuettes are preserved[35]. A common type is Priapus lifting up his garment so as to
form a fold which is filled with fruit, the phallus being visible
beneath. These are the same elements that appear united in the
liknon filled with fruit among which a phallus rises. The liknon
is admirably suited precisely to Priapus and I suspect that this
sacral symbol may have its origin in the cult of Priapus, and

---

[34] Horatius, Sat., i, 8.

[35] See H. Herter, De Priapo, 1932, and his article in the Realenc. d. class. Altertumswissenschaft.

that it has been transferred to Dionysos who stood in a close relation to him. A Priapus is represented on not a few of the monuments belonging to the cult of Bacchus in Italy.[36]

Once the liknon had become a holy symbol it was transferred to other cults. On the gloss defining the practical use of the liknon another follows, saying that the liknon is appropriate for every initiation and sacrifice.[37] Monuments from the Roman age, e. g. the urn published by Countess Lovatelli,[38] show that it was held above the head of the neophyte at the preliminary initiation into the Eleusinian mysteries; it is covered by a cloth but the phallus seems to be lacking. A late notice says that at weddings at Athens it was customary for a boy, carrying thistles with acorns and a liknon filled with bread, to say: "I have escaped the worse and found the better".[39] The custom is first mentioned by the Atticist Pausanias who lived in the reign of the emperor Hadrian. This liknon is not Dionysiac, it is filled with bread.

When the liknon had become a sacred implement used in the mysteries the ancient theologians began to speculate on its significance. Servius relates their explanations at length in his commentary to Vergil's Georgica.[40] "It is a sieve used on the thresh-

---

[36] See below fig. 17 b p. 87 and fig. 21 p. 94. In Samnium images of Bacchus and Priapus were erected together, ILS, 3372/3, *signum Liberi patris et Priapisci;* cf. CIG, vi, 564.

[37] Suidas, Harpokration, Λικνοφόρος· τὸ λίκνον πρὸς πᾶσαν τελετὴν καὶ θυσίαν ἐπιτήδειόν ἐστι. ὁ δὲ τοῦτο φέρων λικνοφόρος λέγεται. Hesych., λικνοφορεῖ· λίκνον στεφανούμενος θρησκεύει.

[38] See further my GGR, i, p. 620 n. 1, second ed. p. 654 n. 2, pl. 43, 2.

[39] Suidas etc. s. v., ἔφυγον κακόν, εὗρον ἄμεινον; cf. above p. 23.

[40] Servius ad Verg. Georg., i, v. 166, *Id est cribrum areale. Mystica autem Iacchi ideo ait, quod Liberi patris sacra ad purgationem animae pertinebant, et sic homines eius mysteriis purgabantur, sicut vannis frumenta purgantur. Hinc est quod dicitur Osiridis membra a Typhone dilaniati Isis cribro superposuisse. Nam idem est Liber pater, in cuius mysteriis vannus est, quia, ut diximus, animas purgat. Unde et Liber ab eo quod liberet dictus, quem Orpheus a Gigantibus dicit esse discerptum. Nonnulli Liberum patrem apud Graecos* Λικμητὴν *dici adserunt; vannus autem apud eos* λικμός *nuncupatur, ubi de more positus esse dicitur, postquam est utero matris editus. Alii mysticam sic accipiunt ut vannum vas vimineum latum dicant, in quod ipsi propter capacitatem congerere rustici primitias frugum soleant et Libero et Liberae sacrum facere; inde mystica. Cf. ibid., ii, v. 388.* Λικνίτην is a conjecture.

ing floors. He calls it 'mystica vannus Iacchi' because the rites of Liber pater pertain to the purification of the soul. Men are purified in his mysteries just as corn is purified by the winnowing-fan. This is why it is said that Isis placed on a sieve the limbs of Osiris after he had been torn to pieces by Typhon. For he is the same as Liber pater in whose mysteries the *vannus* is used, because, as we said, it purifies the soul. That is why Liber (viz. he who makes free) is so named, because he liberates, and Orpheus says that he was torn to pieces by the Giants. Some say that Liber pater is called Likmetes by the Greeks, for *vannus* is called λικμός by them, and he is said to have been placed in it when he was born from his mother's womb. Others interpret the word *mystica* thus, saying that the *vannus* is a large vessel of wickerwork in which, because of its capacity, the peasants used to assemble the firstfruits and make sacrifice to Liber and Libera. Hence it is called 'mystica'."

The elements of this learned explanation are familiar. The new conception of the world, popularized in the Hellenistic age, had transferred the Underworld to the aerial space. The souls ascending in this are purified by the wind, as Virgil says.[41] Likewise a strong wind was needed for cleaning the corn and separating it from the chaff, as described by Homer (see p. 22). This compared admirably with the process by which souls were purified in the air and separated from their evil elements by the wind. The comparison of Dionysos with Osiris, both of whom had been torn to pieces, recurs in a passage of Plutarch to which we shall come back below (pp. 38 f.). The statement in the last sentence that the peasants put firstfruits into a liknon and offered them to Liber and Libera may well be taken from an actual rite and hint at the origin of the liknon filled with fruit. We cannot tell if any of this theological wisdom was imparted to the mystae of Bacchus or to some of them, but on the whole these theological speculations were certainly not of great importance for the Bacchic mysteries as we know them.

---

[41] Vergil, Aen., vi, vv. 740 ff.; references in my GGR, ii, p. 471; add Cumont, Lux perpetua, p. 175 and pp. 208 ff.

38

IV. Dionysos Liknites.

Much more attention has been paid to Dionysos Liknites in modern writings on Dionysos and his religion than in ancient literature. The epithet is in fact rare, occurring only three times. It is found first in Plutarch, who mentions only the epithet Liknites, used here in reference to the child Dionysos. It occurs twice in the Orphic hymns, which were composed in Asia Minor, perhaps at Pergamon,[1] to serve a mystic cult[2] in which Dionysos is especially prominent. Ten of the 87 hymns, which embrace the whole universe, are devoted to him or his followers. In the 52nd hymn, to the Trieterikos, Liknites is but one of many epithets. Much more interesting is the 46th hymn, address-ed to Liknites himself, who is expressly said to be Dionysos. In his explanation of the winnowing-fan Servius confuses this implement and the sieve.[3] λίχνον is a conjecture, but λικμός has the same significance. As to Plutarch, I have always had some qualms when I quoted his information that the Thyiads at Delphi awakened the Liknites,[4] although I did not express them.[5] The passage occurs in a tractate soaked in syncretism, mysticism, and theological speculations, and certainly composed at a late period of Plutarch's life, in the early part of the second century A. D. It is addressed to Klea, the head of the college of the Thyiads, to whom such ideas were not foreign: she was a devotee of the holy rites of Osiris, and not only she herself but also her father and mother.[6] Hence she knows, adds Plutarch, that Dionysos is the same as Osiris and represents the liquid element. Plutarch was himself initiated into the Dionysiac mysteries.

---

[1] See my GGR, ii, pp. 347 and 411.

[2] Most of the hymns end with an invocation of the god to come to the mystae or to the initiation (τελετή).

[3] See above p. 36 with n. 40.

[4] Plutarch, de Iside, p. 365 A, καὶ θύουσιν οἱ Ὅσιοι θυσίαν ἀπόρρητον ἐν τῷ ἱερῷ τοῦ Ἀπόλλωνος, ὅταν αἱ Θυιάδες ἐγείρωσι τὸν Λικνίτην.

[5] See my GGR, i, p. 547, 2nd ed. p. 579, but cf. ii, p. 348.

[6] Plutarch, loc. cit. p. 364 E, ἀρχικλὰ μὲν οὖσαν ἐν Δελφοῖς τῶν Θυιάδων, τοῖς δ' Ὀσιριακοῖς καθωσιωμένην ἱεροῖς ἀπὸ πατρὸς καὶ μητρός.

|The child in the liknon is commonly considered to represent
the vegetation which is awakened in the spring. Parallels to such
an idea, which seems very natural, are adduced: Plutarch relates
how the Phrygians believed that the god sleeps in the winter
and is awakened in summer, and celebrated his going to sleep
and his awakening. He mentions also the Paphlagonian belief
that the god is bound and shut up in the winter, but moves and
is untied in the spring.[7] Galen says that the Bacchants used to
tear snakes asunder at the end of the spring before summer had
commenced,[8] a notice which probably alludes to his native
country, Pergamon, and is not taken from the Cretan archiater
of Neio, Andromachus, whom he quotes. The rhetor Himerius
describes in his flowery language how Dionysos brings the spring
and the Bacchic orgia to the Lydians, who celebrate them in a
frenzy, with dancing, on the shores of the Golden river, i. e.
Paktolos.[9] These parallels are not Greek and therefore less
cogent: they are also embroidered with literary clichés.

It always implies some risk to operate with a detached sentence, one should read it in the context in which it stands.[10]
Plutarch says that the Argives call Dionysos bull-born (βουγενής)
and call him up from the water by the sound of trumpets,
throwing a lamb to Pylaochos (the gate-keeper) into the depths.
They conceal their trumpets in thyrsi, as Socrates said in his
tractate on the Hosioi. The Titanika and the Nyktelia agree
with the so-called dismemberments of Osiris and his returns to
life and rebirths. Likewise in regard to the burials. The Egyp-
tians show tombs of Osiris at many places, as it is said, and the
Delphians believe that the remains of Dionysos lie there near
the oracle. And the Hosioi perform a secret sacrifice in the
temple of Apollo when the Thyiads rouse Him in the liknon
(ὅταν ἐγείρωσι τὸν Λικνίτην).

Reading this passage whole one certainly gets the impression
that Plutarch has in mind not the awakening of a sleeping god

---

[7] Plutarch, De E, p. 389 C and De Iside, p. 378 F resp.
[8] Galen, De antid., i, 6, (xiv, p. 45 Kühn).
[9] Himerius, Orat., iii, 6.
[10] Plutarch, loc. cit. 364 F et seqq.

but the raising of him from the dead. One is instantly reminded of the Orphic doctrine that the child Dionysos was dismembered by the Titans and reborn as the second Dionysos, and this myth is hinted at by the mention of the Titanika and their comparison with the dismemberments, returns to life, and rebirths of Osiris. Whatever the real fact may be in regard to the remains of Dionysos lying at Delphi, it is obvious that they were related to the same myth.

An argument for my opinion that the god aroused by the Thyiads was not the god of vegetation, awakening every spring, but the god ascending from the realm of the dead, is the 53rd Orphic hymn, addressed to the god of the trieteric orgia.[11] It is not much later than the tractate of Plutarch. It reads in translation: "I call upon Bacchos, appearing every second year, the chthonian Dionysos, aroused together with fair-haired nymphs, who, reposing in the holy house of Persephone, sleeps a holy Bacchic time of two years, but when he again arouses the trieteric revel he turns to a hymn with his fair-girdled nurses, now lulling to sleep, now arousing the times as the seasons wheel by". This god is not the god awakened every spring but the god of the orgia, which were celebrated every second year, and he rises from the realm of the dead, where he sleeps a time of two years. The biennial period is contradictory to the yearly awakening of vegetation.

---

[11] Hymn. orph., 53, Ἀμφιετοῦς.

Ἀμφιετῆ καλέω Βάκχον, χθόνιον Διόνυσον,
ἐγρόμενον κούραις ἅμα νύμφαις εὐπλοκάμοισιν,
ὃς παρὰ Περσεφόνης ἱεροῖσι δόμοισιν ἰαύων
κοιμίζει τριετῆρα χρόνον, Βακχήιον ἁγνόν.
αὐτὸς δ' ἡνίκα τὸν τριετῆ πάλι κῶμον ἐγείρῃ,
εἰς ὕμνον τρέπεται σὺν εὐζώνοισι τιθήναις
εὐνάζων κινῶν τε χρόνους ἐνὶ κυκλάσιν ὥραις.

The words ἀμφιετής and τριετήρ refer evidently to the biennial period of the orgia and cannot here be translated with Liddell and Scott 'yearly' and 'of three years' respectively. In the latter case it is the usual inclusive reckoning. The translation of the last line is due to Professor Rose. He adds: "The sense is that Dionysos, by staying in the realm of Persephone or quitting it, causes times of (or possibly alternating years of) inactivity and the stir of festival". Abel emends to read χορούς for χρόνους, which would give a good sense.

Considering the text of Plutarch and its age more closely, I do not find my earlier treatment of it[12] satisfactory. We do not know much of the beliefs and the rites that imply beliefs of the Dionysiac mysteries of the Hellenistic and Roman age, but it is necessary to try and see how far what we know agrees with the above considerations.

The passage in Plutarch quoted above refers in its beginning to the mysteries at Lerna, where it was said that Dionysos descended through the Alcyonian lake to Hades to fetch his mother Semele.[13] The same tale was told at Troizen,[14] and Plutarch says of the ennaeteric festival Herois at Delphi that it contains chiefly a mystic tale which the Thyiads know, but that from what is done one would evidently guess at the bringing up of Semele.[15] This passage is worth noticing for our purpose, for it proves that the rites of the Thyiads had at this time become deeply infected by myths and mysticism. An inscription from the time of Caracalla found on Rhodes speaks of a player of the hydraulic organ who aroused the god and of his two ascents.[16] They ought to be his rebirth after his being dismembered by the Titans and his ascent with Semele. This is not much, but all of it refers to the ascent of Dionysos from the realm of the dead, nothing to the awakening of the vegetation god in the spring.

The ancient interpreters of the myths and cults of Dionysos do not help much. To them he is the god of wine and they mix this up with Orphic ideas. Diodorus devotes many chapters in the end of his third book to Dionysos. He refers the myth of his dismemberment to viticulture and wine-pressing, adding that the Orphic poems and the mysteries agree with this.[17] Probably he has the orgia and the omophagia in mind. The same ideas recur in Cornutus[18] and gave rise to a mystic conception of the

---

[12] See my Minoan-Myc. Religion, pp. 494, 2nd ed. pp. 565.

[13] Paus., ii, 37, 5; see my Griech. Feste, p. 288.

[14] Paus., ii, 31, 2.

[15] Plutarch, quaest. graecae, p. 293 C.

[16] Österreichische Jahreshefte, vii, 1904, pp. 92; see below p. 64 with n. 107.

[17] Diodorus, iii, 62, σύμφωνα δὲ τούτοις εἶναι τὰ δηλούμενα διὰ τῶν Ὀρφικῶν ποιημάτων καὶ τὰ παρεισαγόμενα κατὰ τὰς τελετάς.

[18] Cornutus, Theologia graeca, p. 58 Lang.

wine-pressing.[19] If or how far such ideas were taken up by the mysteries of the age is unknown.[20]

Much more relevant and agreeing with the rôle of the dying and rising Dionysos in the mysteries is the fact that Dionysiac cult associations paid attention to the burials of their members. We come back to this topic below pp. 65 f.

Having pointed out this belief of the mystae of Dionysos, we come back to Dionysos Liknites in the Orphic hymns. In the 52nd hymn to the Trieterikos, Liknites is but one of many epithets. Much more interesting is the 46th hymn, addressed to Liknites himself, who is expressly said to be Dionysos. The first verses refer to the god of the orgia; the last are important, for they say that, through the will of Zeus brought to the noble Persephone, he was reared up, dear to the immortal gods. Here his relation to the world of the dead appears again, as it does in his mysteries and in the Orphic hymns in which he is constantly associated with the deities of the Nether World.[21]

Finally Proklos hints at the Liknites without mentioning his name.[22] He speaks of Hipta, a goddess from Asia Minor, to

---

[19] See my paper 'Die Anthesterien und die Aiora', Eranos, xv, 1916, pp. 191, reprinted in my Opuscula selecta, i, pp.156, and my 'Symbolisme etc.' (cited p. 23 n. 10) pp. 224.

[20] The words of Justinus Martyr, Apol., i, 54, in a very sweeping account of Dionysos: καὶ οἶνον ἐν τοῖς μυστηρίοις αὐτοῦ ἀναγράφουσι, are not good evidence for mystery rites. They refer to the ideas in Diodorus. I cannot believe, as Kerényi does, that from the first Dionysos was the god of wine and that certain Orphic myths and rites refer to viticulture; see in the last instance his lecture 'Un sacrificio Dionisiaco', printed in the Italian periodical Dioniso, xiv, 1951, pp. 3. Old vintage festivals, e.g. the Oschophoria and the Staphylodromoi at the Karneia, were not attached to Dionysos. He was at first a vegetation god and connected with the tree cult but not especially the god of wine.

[21] In the 30th Orphic hymn Dionysos is called Eubouleus, who in these hymns is a god of the Nether World, and according to the Orphic myth he is said to be a son of Zeus and Persephone. In the 42nd hymn to Mise he is said to be σπέρμα Εὐβουλῆος and in the 52nd hymn to Trieterikos he is given the epithet Eubouleus, likewise Adonis in the 56th hymn. Cp. also the 53rd hymn quoted above p. 40.

[22] Proklos, in Plat. Timaeum, i, p. 407 Diehl, = Kern, Orphic. fragm., no. 199: λίκνον ἐπὶ τῆς κεφαλῆς θεμένη καὶ δράκοντι αὐτὸ περιστέψασα τὸ(ν) κραδιαῖον ὑποδέχεται Διόνυσον. τὸν instead of τό is a correction of Lobeck's.

whom the 49th Orphic hymn is addressed and who is mentioned in the 48th, v. 8. Proklos says that she put the liknon on her head, surrounded it with a serpent,[23] and received the κραδιαῖος Dionysos in it. This is a rare word, used by the Neoplatonists. Liddell and Scott translate "belonging to the heart", deriving the adjective from the Doric form κραδία, and this is right in view of the other passages in which the word is found and of the context of Proklos. He says that Hipta is called the Soul of All, perhaps because of the swift motion, of which she is the cause, and after the quoted words he proceeds to say that she receives the cosmic intellect (ἐγκόσμιον νοῦν). Dionysos proceeds from the thigh of Zeus into her, becomes part of her, and carries her to the Intelligible and to his own source. In the hymn to the Sun, I, v. 6, the same Proklos says of Helios: κόσμου κραδιαῖον ἔχων ἐριφεγγέα κύκλον.[24] Dionysos is the heart, the centre of the world, like the Sun in this hymn, like the second person of the Trinity, the Son, in a hymn of the neoplatonizing Christian Synesios,[25] and like the Sun again in the speech on the Sungod by the emperor Julian.

---

[23] Of course serpents belong to the old cult of Dionysos, see e.g. the vase mentioned p. 24, but in Proklos the singular and the verb are noticeable: Hipta surrounded the liknon with a serpent. As the whole passage is soaked in Neoplatonic speculations, it may be permitted to think of the οὐροβόρος ὄφις which often appears as a symbol of the world which renews itself.

[24] Proklos, Hymnus in Solem, vv. 5,

> μεσσατίην γὰρ ἔχων ὑπὲρ αἴθερος ἕδρην·
> καὶ κόσμου κραδιαῖον ἔχων ἐριφεγγέα κύκλον·
> πάντα τεῆς ἔπλησας ἐγερσινόοιο προνοίης.

[25] Synesios, Hymnus ii, (v, Terzaghi), vv. 25:

> μία παγά, μία ῥίζα,   κραδιαῖόν τι λόχευμα
> τριφαὴς ἔλαμψε μορφά,   σοφία κοσμοτεχνῖτις
> ἵνα γὰρ βυθὸς πατρῷος,   ἑνοτήσιόν τε φέγγος
> τόθε καὶ κύδιμος υἱός.   ἁγίας ἔλαμψε πνοιᾶς.

Fitzgerald translates: "offspring as it were of the heart". "Von der Freude am jungen Tageslicht schwingt sich der Hymnus empor zu der Quelle alles Lichts, der extramundanen Gottheit jenseits der achten Fixsternensphäre". "Die Trinitätslehre selbst ist freilich im Grunde nur eine Spielart der Spekulation, die wir neuplatonisch nennen, und die Gedanken ebenso wie die Bilder, die das Unvorstellbare erläutern sollen, führen auf Iamblich und die chaldäischen Orakel zurück." Wilamowitz, 'Die Hymnen des Proklos und des Synesios', Sitz.-ber. der

Cosmological speculations, well known in regard to the Sun
as the centre and the leader of the Universe, recur in the above-
quoted passage of Proklos referring to Dionysos. But he is
carried in the liknon, he is the Child who, according to the
Orphic myth, was destined by Zeus to be Lord of the Universe,
and from this myth the Neoplatonist, whose Bible the Orphic
poems were, borrowed the epithet κραδιαῖος. For the myth
told how Dionysos' heart was saved by Athena, when the Titans
dismembered the Child, and was brought to Zeus. So the second
Dionysos was born.

The mask of the bearded and ivy-crowned Dionysos seen in
the liknon on the Vlasto chous has nothing to do with the
Liknites recorded in the Roman age, nor has the liknon on this
vase anything to do with the mystica vannus Iacchi. The liknon
has no symbolic value on early monuments; but as new Dionysiac mysteries, other than the old orgia of the Maenads, arose in
the Hellenistic age, they needed symbols and took up the liknon,
which, filled with fruit and containing a phallus, served as a
symbol of purification and fertility. Orphic myths and ideas are
apparent in the arousing of the Liknites by the Thyiads at
Delphi, mentioned by Plutarch. Finally the Neoplatonist Proklos
seized upon the Dionysos in the liknon, conceiving him as Lord
of the Universe, which, according to the Orphics, Zeus had
destined him to be. The little we know about the ideas of the
Dionysiac mysteries of the Roman age shows no trace of a vegetation god; they were concerned with the ascent of Dionysos from
the Underworld and they looked after the burials of their
members. The sarcophagi show that the hope of a joyous afterlife was essential to them. In view of this fact the question may
be asked, if the phallus, which takes so prominent a place in
the liknon, does simply signify fertility, of whose importance
the urbanized people unlike the old agricultural people had no
real understanding. May it not rather have symbolized the life-
giving power?

Phalli were erected on tombs in the neighbourhood of Smyrna

---

preuss. Akad. d. Wiss. Berlin, 1907, p. 284. Professor Rose reminds me of Pru-
dentius, Cathem., ix, 10: *corde natus ex parentis ante mundi exordium.*

and in Phrygia[26] and were used as tops of tomb monuments in Bithynia and Paphlagonia.[27] A single example comes from Macedonia near Strymon.[28] The custom was not unknown in Greece. A white lekythos shows a big phallus as a tomb monument.[29] This use of the phallus may be explained by its life-giving power, like the eggs and seeds which were laid down in the tomb. In regard to the frequency of this use in Northwestern Asia Minor and the popularity of Dionysiac mysteries in those areas it is perhaps not too rash to suggest that the use of the phallus in the Dionysiac mysteries may have received an impulse from that quarter. In a certain sense this would agree with the hope of a joyous afterlife. We may perhaps be allowed to guess that the symbols of the Dionysiac mysteries, promising immortality, to which Plutarch refers in a passage quoted below p. 123 n. 15, were precisely the liknon with its contents; for no other symbols of these mysteries are known to us, and the representations show that the initiation consisted in revealing just this symbol.

V. The Greek Lands in the Roman Age.

After this digression we take up the thread from our second chapter, adding to the testimonies of the Dionysiac mysteries in Asia Minor and adjacent lands during the Hellenistic age those from the Roman age. We remark, however, that the liknon is mentioned but rarely. A λικναφόρος occurs in an enumeration of functionaries from Apollonia in Thrace,[1] and three in the

---

[26] Athen. Mitt., xxiv, 1899, pp. 7 ff.; Herter in the Realenc. d. class. Altertumswiss., xix, pp. 1728 ff.

[27] Archäol. Anzeiger, 1939, pp. 171 ff. with fig. 40.

[28] Ibid. 1940, p. 280.

[29] British Museum Quarterly, iii, pp. 7 ff.

[1] CIG, 2052. IG, vii, 3392 from Chaeronea, ἐλε[ικνο]φόρησε Σάτυρος is a supplement and the cult is doubtful.

inscription of Agrippinilla. The reason may be that the Dionysiac mysteries in Asia Minor were attached to or influenced by old cults. The liknon had to emigrate to the West in order to be fully appreciated as a sacred symbol.

The materials for our study consist of inscriptions, which with some few remarkable exceptions do no more than mention the functionaries. These lists will be the basis of our research. However, there are two very extensive and important inscriptions of which something must be said first. One is the inscription of the Iobacchi from Athens,[2] found at the place which according to Dörpfeld was the old site of the sanctuary of Dionysos ἐν λίμναις. It is dated in the archonship of Ar(rius) Epaphroditus, but his year is not known. Aurelius Nicomachus, who had been vice priest 17 years and priest 23 years, ceded his office to Claudius Herodes and accepted appointment by him as vice priest. Herodes must have been a prominent man, but he was not the famous rhetor. Maass has proved that he was his son, or more probably his grandson, who lived in the early part of the third century A. D.[3] The statutes were older, formulated by two earlier priests of the association. Their main contents are rules for the admission of members and for maintaining good order at the banquets. The cult of the Iobacchi is not said to include mysteries, but it is closely connected with the Dionysiac mysteries both by its hierarchy and by certain ritual performances.

The second great inscription is that of Agrippinilla, found probably at Torre Nova not far south of Rome and now in the Metropolitan Museum in New York.[4] It is engraved on a base

---

[2] IG, ii², 1368; ŞIG, 1109. First published by Wide, Athen. Mitt., xix, 1894, pp. 248 ff., reprinted and commented upon by E. Maass, Orpheus, 1895, pp. 14 ff. His attempt to prove an Orphic character of the association is not convincing.

[3] Maass, loc. cit. pp. 32 ff.

[4] Published with an excellent commentary by A. Vogliano and F. Cumont, La grande iscrizione bacchica del Metropolitan Museum, Amer. Journ. of Archaeology, xxxvii, 1933, pp. 215 ff.; cf. my paper, En marge de la grande inscription bacchique du Metropolitan Museum, Studi e materiali di storia delle religioni, x, 1934, pp. 1 ff., reprinted in my Opuscula selecta, ii, pp. 524 ff.

that supported a statue of Agrippinilla, erected by the mystae whose names and functions are written on the three sides. The first three letters of the name of Agrippinilla have vanished,[5] but Vogliano has established that she was the wife of M. Gavius Squilla Gallicanus, consul in 150 A. D. and proconsul in Asia about 165 A. D. His son Cethegus was his legatus. Agrippinilla was a descendant of Pompeius Theophanes from Mytilene, and the family had possessions on the island of Lesbos. She had come to know the Dionysiac mysteries during her stay in Asia Minor and had taken them with her to Rome. It is a family association. Other names of the family are found among the high functionaries, while the rest are members of her household, freedmen and slaves. Of some four hundred persons registered more than three hundred have Greek names, seventy Latin, very few barbarian, none Semitic or Egyptian. Most of the names are such as are proper to slaves but the persons may also be freedmen. The titles of the functionaries and members recur in inscriptions from Asia Minor. Consequently this inscription has its place among the Dionysiac cults of Asia Minor and is valuable for its exuberant hierarchy, which is parallelled in other inscriptions from Asia Minor.

In the Hellenistic age mysteries were sometimes connected with old cults of Dionysos;[6] further examples come from the Roman age. At Ephesus the mysteries of Demeter and Dionysos Phleus were united.[7] Dionysos Phleus is an old god whose name is variously written.[8] At Erythrae a pannychis was celebrated in honour of the same god.[9] The mystae of Dionysos Breiseus at Smyrna seem to have been an association of actors which posed

---

[5] ['Αγρ]ιππεινίλλαν τὴν ἱέρειαν μύσται οἱ ὑπογεγραμμένοι.

[6] See above pp. 8 ff.

[7] BMI, iii, 2, 595; Quandt, p. 161: ἱερατεύοντος διὰ βίου τῶν πρὸ πόλεως Δημητριαστῶν καὶ Διονύσου Φλέω μυστῶν Τίτου Αὐρηλίου Πλουτάρχου, ἱεροφαντοῦντος Πο. Κλαυδίου 'Αριστοφάνους, ἐπιμελητοῦ δὲ τῶν μυστηρίων Σατορνείλου δὶς τοῦ 'Ονήσωνος.

[8] Φλεύς, Φλέος, Φλοιός, see my GGR, i, p. 552 n. 5, 2nd ed. p. 584 n. 8.

[9] Österr. Jahreshefte, xiii, 1910, p. 34 No. 5; Quandt, p. 150, [Διονύσ]ωι Φλεῖ ἐκ παννυχίδος κτλ.

as a mystery association.[10] One may suspect that the mystae of Dionysos Setaneios who honour an Asiarch were also an association of actors:[11] the inscription comes from Teos, which was the seat of the Dionysiac technitae. More in earnest was another association, the σακηφόροι mystae of the ancestral god Dionysos Koresites who honoured the emperor Commodus.[12] Koresos is a hill and a suburb at Ephesus. σάκος is a coarse cloth of hair, especially goats' hair, and also a garment or sack made of this cloth. Such a cloth worn by the mystae of Dionysos is peculiar. The explanation may perhaps be that the Maenads sometimes wore a goatskin instead of a fawnskin.[13] Aeschylus speaks thus of the νεβρίς and the goat was a victim of the Bacchants.[14] The garment of goats' hair may be a last relic of the goatskins worn in the orgia.

It was noted above pp. 9 f. that the ancestral god of the Pergamene kings, Dionysos Kathegemon, had mysteries during their reign. These mysteries are also recorded in some inscriptions from the Roman age.[15] The members of the association were called βουκόλοι and performed dances of which we shall have more to say below (p. 59); they celebrated mysteries every second year. This is an indication that the cult was in some manner connected with the old orgia. A branch of this cult is found at

---

[10] CIG, 3190, ἡ ἱερὰ σύνοδος τῶν περὶ τὸν Βρισέα Διόνυσον τεχνιτῶν καὶ μυστῶν; 3173, in the reign of Titus, mentions entrance fees and πατρομύσται, so too 3195; 3176 is a letter of thanks from M. Aurelius. Collected by Quandt, pp. 147 f.

[11] Le Bas Waddington, 106; Quandt, p. 155 ..... τὸν 'Ασιάρχην οἱ το[ῦ Ση-τα]νείου θεοῦ Διονύσο[υ μύσται] τὸν ἐκ προγόνων εὐεργ[έτην]...

[12] Österr. Jahreshefte, xxiii, 1926, Beibl. p. 265; SEG, iv, 522, οἱ τοῦ προπάτορος θεοῦ Διονύσου Κορησείτου σακηφόροι μύσται.

[13] Hesych., τραγηφόροι· αἱ κόραι Διονύσῳ ὀργιάζουσαι τραγῆν περιήπτοντο.

[14] Hesych. and Suidas, αἰγίζειν· διασπᾶν ἐκ μεταφορᾶς · παρ' ὃ καὶ τὸ αἰγίζεσθαι ἀπὸ τῶν καταιγίδων, Αἰσχύλος. ὁ δ' αὐτὸς ἐν 'Ηδωνοῖς καὶ τὰς νεβρίδας οὕτω λέγει. Cf. also Dionysos μελαναιγίς and the word τραγῳδία, whose origin is doubtful in spite of a lively discussion. See my paper, Der Ursprung der Tragödie, N. Jahrb. f. klass. Altertumswiss., xxvii, 1911, pp. 688 ff., reprinted in my Opuscula selecta, i, pp. 133.

[15] Collected by Quandt, pp. 123 f., and treated by Ohlemutz, pp. 110 ff., cited abote p. 10 n. 22.

Philadephia,[16] a town founded by the inhabitants of Pergamon.

In the mysteries at Lerna in Argolis, which flourished in Late Antiquity, Dionysos was joined with Demeter.[17] An inscription on the base of a statue, representing a man named Archelaos, says that it was dedicated to these gods and calls him a Bacchos, i. e. a mystes of Dionysos.[18] At Panamara in Caria an association had the unusual name of Ἰακχισταί, and the inscription mentions mystae and a mystagogue.[19]

Finally two inscriptions mention Dionysiac mysteries but add nothing to our knowledge of them. Both belong to the late age in which men were eager to be initiated into several mysteries. One is a tomb epigram from Thebes, which mentions a man who had been initiated into the mysteries of Dionysos as well as of Demeter.[20] The other, an epigram from Athens, is written for a child of seven years.[21]

The adherents of the Dionysiac mysteries were organized in

---

[16] Inscriptions collected by Quandt, pp. 179 ff.

[17] See my GGR, ii, p. 337.

[18] IG, iv, 666; Kaibel, 821, Βάκχῳ με βάκχον καὶ προσυμναίᾳ θεῶι στάσαντο Δηοῦς ἐν κατηρεφεῖ δόμωι κτλ.

[19] Benndorff und Niemann, Reisen in Lykien und Karien, i, p. 156 No. 35, lines b 16, b 18, and a 9, resp.

[20] Peek, 694, probably third century A. D.,

βουλευτὴν Θηβῶν ἀρχὰς τελέσαντα πόληι
Δήμητρος μύστην ὤμοις κάδον ἀείροντα,
αιχιπα τοὔνομ' ἔχον[τα πολυστεφάνοιο] δὲ Βάχχ[ου]
...θνεοκλόνων κλει[νῶν] τελ[ετ]ῶν νεο[φάν]την κτλ.

Unhappily many letters in lines 4 and 5 are badly worn. The word νεοφάντης is only found in Hymn. orph. 4, 9, κλῦθ' ἐπάγων ζωὴν ὁσίαν μύστηι νεοφάντηι, and must signify "neophyte".

[21] Peek, 1029; IG, ii², 11674, vv. 9 ff.

καὶ γάρ μ' Εὐμ[όλποιο] θυήπολοι εἰρεσιώνην
τεύξαντες [μεγάλην ὤ]πασαν εὐκλείην·
στέμμα δέ [μοι πλέξαντο] Διωνύσου θιασῶται,
πυρφόρ[ου ἐν Δηοῦς μύστι]κά τ' ἐξετέλουν.

Probably second century or later. That the boy took part in various cults reminds us of the boyhood of Cyprian in the Confessio of S. Cyprian (See my paper, Harvard Theol. Rev., xl, 1947, pp. 167 ff.). Unhappily the inscription is badly damaged and the supplements must be taken with caution. It would be interesting if the agrarian rite of carrying the eiresione took place in the groups, like the Maenads who took part in the orgia, but the old word "thiasos" was seldom used.[22] The common word is σπεῖρα, Latin *spira*, which also signifies a tactical unit of the army, Latin *manipulus*. The designation κατάζωσμα is found in an inscription from Philadelphia.[23] In the inscription cited from Acmonia the "first" thiasus is mentioned: hence there was a higher organisation comprising two or more thiasi, just as in the old orgia of the Maenads. An inscription from Cyzicus seems to indicate a like arrangement, since it speaks of τῶν πρώτων Βάκχων Κυνοσουρειτῶν.[24] When sometimes a local name is added it may be supposed that the σπεῖρα belonged to a more comprehensive organization. Two altars are dedicated to Διονύσῳ Καθηγεμόνι καὶ τῆι Μιδαπεδειτῶν σπείρηι.[25] Midapedeion is a place in the neighbourhood of Pergamon.[26] A σπεῖρα Βραχυλειτῶν is mentioned at Erythrae.[27] A dedication to Βρόμιος Παχοριτῶν comes from Pergamon.[28] At Philadelphia διάταξις and κατάζωσμα seem to refer to groups within an association.

A Baccheion of the Asiani is mentioned at Perinthus,[29] and at Dionysopolis in Thrace likewise a σπεῖρα τῶν Ἀσιανῶν,[30] while a Latin inscription from Dacia records the names of the Asiani of a spira.[31] It seems that people from Asia Minor when emigrating to Thrace formed a special group introducing their mysteries. This is confirmed by two inscriptions from Callatis in Thrace, set up by a thiasus in the first century A. D. In the

Eleusinian mysteries; it belongs otherwise to the cult of Apollo. Fire-carriers are mentioned in the inscription of Agrippinilla, though here the word may simply signify torch-bearer. But the half of the verse including the name of the goddess is a supplement.

[22] In Acmonia in Phrygia and Callatis, see below p. 63 n. 94 and 51 n. 33 resp.

[23] Quandt, p. 179 f., see below p. 55.

[24] CIG, 3679; Quandt, p. 130.

[25] I Perg., 319, 320; Quandt, p. 123.

[26] Ohlemutz, loc. cit. p. 110.

[27] Österr. Jahreshefte, xiii, 1910, p. 48 No. 13; Quandt, p. 150.

[28] Cited below, p. 62 n. 92.

[29] IGRom., i, 787, τὸν τελαμῶνα (stone with inscription) τῷ Βαχχείῳ Ἀσιανῶν·

[30] Rev. des études grecques, lxv, 1952, Bull. épigraphique No. 100.

[31] See below p. 54 n. 55.

first the members decide to build a temple to the god (viz. Dionysos), and a list of the subscribers follows.[32] The second is an honorary decree which mentions the "foreign Dionysia".[33] Two inscriptions from Rome, set up by leaders of a spira, and one from Puteoli, mentioning priests and orgiophantae,[34] seem to show that the mysteries of Asia Minor also reached Italy; the names given in these inscriptions are Greek.

The association of Agrippinilla consisted of her family and house-folk (p. 47); another family association is known from Thasos[35] and a third from Malko-Tirnavo in Bulgaria.[36] In the Hellenistic age an association was often named after its head, who probably had formed it, and this happens also with the Dionysiac associations.[37]

The thiasi of the old orgia had a single leader, e. g. Agaue in the Bacchants of Euripides, or Klea at Delphi in the time of Plutarch. The new Dionysiac mysteries are distinguished by an elaborate hierarchy, with functionaries and members of varying degrees. We must enumerate these titles as recorded by the inscriptions, for our knowledge of the character of the Dionysiac mysteries among the Greeks of the Roman age is founded upon them. The longest list is that of the inscription of Agrippinilla. She herself was the priestess, viz. the head of the association. The list commences with [Μαχ]ρεῖνος ἥρως, an enigmatical title.[38]

---

[32] Dacia, i, 1924, No. 1, pp. 126 ff.

[33] Ibid. No. 2, pp. 139 ff., ἐνγράψαι δὲ τοὺς θιασείτας τὸ ψήφισμα τοῦτο εἰς τελαμῶνα λευκοῦ λίθου ἕως μηνὸς Λυκήου τῶν ξενικῶν Διονυσίων εἰς τὸν ἐπιφανέστατον τοῦ μυχοῦ τόπον. According to the dating in line 1 the festival was biennial: μηνὸς Διονυσίου ἐν τριετηρίδι.

[34] See below p. 54 n. 53 and 54.

[35] IG, xii: 8, 387, τὸ ἱερώτατον νέον Βαχχῖον τὸν ἀξιολογώτατον Ἰούν(ιον) Λαβ(έριον) Μακεδόνα [τὸ]ν ἑαυτῶν ἱεροφά[ντη]ν μηθὲν ἀντεστ....

[36] Österr. Jahreshefte, xxix, 1937, Beiblatt, p. 165 f., square altar. βωμὸν τόνδ' ἀνέθηκα θεῷ Διὶ τῷ Διονύσῳ Λυκομήδης Χρήστου ἱερεὺς Βαχχείου μεγάλοιο ὑπὲρ ἐμῶν παίδων καὶ τειμῆς ἧς λάχον αὐτὸς καὶ μυστῶν ἰδίων οὓς σῷζε μάκαρ Διόνυσε.

[37] Bull. corr. hell., iv, 1880, p. 164 No. 21 from Teos, μύσται οἱ σὺν Ἀθηνοδότωι Μητροδώρου; ibid. xxiv, 1900, p. 317, from the village of Alistrati near Philippi in Thrace, οἱ περεὶ Ῥοῦφον Ζείπα μύστε Βότρυος Διονύσου μύ[στ]άρχῃ Ῥο]ύφῳ τῷ εὐερ[γέτῃ].

[38] In my paper, cited p. 46 n. 4, p. 2, I suggested that Macrinus had paid his

Then follow: [Κηθ]ηγίλλα δαδοῦχος, 7 priests of whom two Orphiti, Macrinus, Tertullus, and Celsus, and two priestesses both named Maliola. These functionaries belong to the noble family, whereas the names that follow are not aristocratic except one, and are chiefly Greek: ἱεροφάντης Ἀγαθόπους, θεοφόροι Gallicanus and Dionysius, ὑπουργὸς καὶ σειληνόκοσμος Serenos, κισταφόροι 3 women, ἀρχιβούκολοι 3 men, βουκόλοι ἱεροί 7 men, ἀρχιβάσσαροι 2 men, ἀμφιθαλεῖς (probably boys), λικναφόροι 3 women, φαλλοφόρος 1 woman, πυρφόροι 2 men, ἱερομνήμων 1 man, ἀρχινεανίσκοι 1 (in spite of the plural), ἀρχιβάσσαραι 4 women, βουκόλοι 11 men, ἀπὸ καταζώσεως 89 men and women, βάκχοι ἀπὸ καταζώσεως 15, βάκχαι ἀπὸ καταζώσεως 3, ἱεροὶ βάκχοι more than 100; then comes a gap in which βάκχοι and perhaps ἱεραὶ βάκχαι were enumerated, 2 ἀντροφύλακες, more than 44 βάκχοι, and 23 male and female σειγηταί.

The statutes of the Iobacchi come next in extent and mention the following functionaries: ἱερεύς, ἀνθιερεύς, ἀρχίβακχος, προστάτης, ἱερεῖς, βουκολικός, ταμίας, γραμματεύς, εὔκοσμος, ἵπποι, ἱεροὶ παῖδες, ἰόβακχος. In the mysteries of Dionysos Kathegemon in Pergamon an inscription lists 18 βουκόλοι, 2 ὑμνοδιδάσκαλοι, 2 σειληνοί, 1 χορηγός;[39] another 12 χορεύσαντες βουκόλοι, 1 διαταξί[αρχος], 1 ἀρχιβούκολος, 13 βουκόλοι.[40] In the branch at Philadelphia a ἱεροφάντης and an ἀρχιβούκολος [τῆς σπ]είρης are mentioned.[41]   The hierophant of Dionysos Kathegemon is also mentioned in another inscription[42] and a third honours

contribution but died before the monument was erected. Cumont objected and advanced the opinion that he was a high functionary of the association: see his paper cited above p. 46 n. 4, pp. 237 ff. Miss Guarducci, Heros nell' età imperiale romana, Atti del III congresso nazionale di studi romani, 1935, iv, pp. 328 ff., has collected examples, showing that in these times living men were called ἥρωες, cf. also my GGR, ii, p. 136 n. 4, but that is exceptional and the term does not designate them as functionaries. The invocation of the Elean women, ἥρω Διόνυσε, is not relevant in this case; cf. my GGR, i, p. 538 n. 4, 2nd ed. p. 571 n. 3.

39 I Perg., 485; SIG, 1115; Quandt, p. 123.
40 Athen. Mitt., xxiv, 1899, p. 179 No. 31; Quandt, p. 123; cf. ibid. p. 180 = I Perg., 486 a.
41 K. Buresch, Aus Lydien, 1898, p. 11 No. 8; Quandt, p. 179 f.
42 Athen. Mitt., xx, 1895, p. 243; Quandt, p. 179.

a man, τὸν ἐκ τῆς περὶ τὸν Καθηγεμόνα Διόνυσον μύστην.[43] In the united mysteries of Demeter and Dionysos Phleus at Ephesus we find a priest, a hierophant, and an epimelete of the mysteries,[44] and in another much mutilated inscription θυρσοφό-ροι, βουκόλοι, βάσσαραι.[45] A remarkable inscription from Magnesia ad Maeandrum, to which we come back below pp. 65 f., mentions an ἀρχιμύστης, an ἄππας Διονύσου, a priestess and στεφανηφόρος, a ἱεροφάντης, a female ὑπότροφος, and another ἄππας. At Apollonia in Thrace we have the list: λικναφό-ρος, βουκόλος, ἑστία[ρχος], κρατηριακός, ἀρχιμύσ[της],[46] at Abdera an ἀρχιβούκολος,[47] and at Thessalonike a γαλακτοφόρος.[48] Below

---

[43] J. Keil und A. v. Premerstein, Bericht über eine Reise in Lydien und der südlichen Aeolis, Denkschriften, Akad. Wien, liii, 1908, p. 28 No. 42; Quandt, p. 179.

[44] BMI, 595; Quandt, p. 161, text above p. 47 n. 7.

[45] BMI, 602; Quandt, p. 161.

[46] CIG, 2052. Καρνεάδης Ἥρα . . .

. . . . δώρου λικναφόρος

. . . . ο . ορου βουκόλος

Φα. . . Ἔκδικος Πωσειδωνίου ἑστία[ρχος]

Νικηφόρος

Ἀλέξανδρος Ἀρισταινέτου κρατηριακός

Τέρτιος [Κ]ρίσ[π]ου ἀρχιμύσ[της]

26 names follow of wich two female.

[47] Bull. corr. hell., lxii, 1938, pp. 51 ff. Γ. Κάσσιος Σέξτος ἀρχιβούκολος θεῷ Διονύσῳ καὶ τοῖς συνμύσταις ἐκ τῶν ἰδίων τὸ μάγαρον ἐποίησεν. The μάγαρον is to be understood as a Dionysiac grotto. This inscription proves that the inscription of an altar, published ibid. xxxvii, 1913, p. 97 No. 7, which has been treated by L. Robert, Inscription de Thessalonique, Mélanges Bidez, 1934, ii, pp. 795 ff., belongs neither to the cult of Mithras nor to that of the Magna Mater, but as Cumont suggested, Amer. J. of Archaeology, xxxvii, 1933, p. 259 n. 2 (cf. Edson, Harvard Theol. Review, xli, 1948, p. 180 f.), to that of Dionysos. The inscription reads: ὁ ἀρχιμαγ . . ευς καὶ ἀρχινεωκόρος καὶ πατὴρ σπηλ-λέου καὶ Αὐρ. Σωσίπατρα ἡ γαλακτοφόρος, κισταφορήσασα(ν) ἔτη λ' τὸν βωμὸν ἐκ τῶν ἰδίων ἀνέθηκαν. Robert's supplement μαγ[αρ]εύς is right.

[48] Cumont, loc. cit., p. 259 n. 2, discusses the γαλακτοφόρος and says that she is incomprehensible. I do not think so. It is often said that milk streamed forth from the earth at the orgia, and from the grotto in the procession of Ptolemy Philadelphos milk flowed as well as wine. She may be an old reminiscence. Moreover one may recall the significance of milk in late theological speculation. The new-born and the neophyte were fed with milk. References in my paper, Astrale Unsterblichkeit und kosmische Mystik, Numen, i, 1954, p. 108 f.

a Sibylline oracle in an inscription from Perinthus the names of
an ἀρχιβούκολος, an ἀρχιμυστῶν, and a σπείραρχος are read.[49]
In the dedication at the Baccheion of the Asiani at Perinthus a
ἡγεμών, a ἱερομνήμων, an ἀρχιμύστης and a priest are mentioned.[50] At Attaleia in Phrygia a ναρθηκοφόρος is honoured by
his family and the σπεῖρα.[51] A very mutilated inscription from
Thasos speaks of fellow-mystae.[52]

The suggestion made above that these mysteries came from
Asia Minor to Italy is supported by the titles and Greek names
in certain inscriptions. An official who is both dadouchos and
spirarches is mentioned in Rome,[53] a spira at Cora, priests and
orgiophantae at Puteoli,[54] and an inscription from Clausenburg
in Dacia lists the names of the Asiani and the spirarches.[55]
Finally a number of titles, some of them Greek, occur in an
inscription from Nicopolis ad Istrum of 227 A. D., enumerating
nomina Bacchii vernaculorum.[56]

---

[49] Rhein. Mus., xxxiv, 1879, p. 211, χρησμὸς Σιβύλλης· ἐπὰν δ' ὁ Βάκχος
εὐάσας πλησ[θήσεται, τό]τ' αἷμα καὶ πῦρ καὶ κόνις μιγήσεται. Σπέλλιος Εὐήθης
ἀρχιβούκολος, Ἡρακλείδου Ἀλεξάνδρου ἀρχιμυστοῦντος, Ἀλέξανδρος σπείραρχος,
four names follow.

[50] IGRom., i, 787, from the reign of the emperor Septimius Severus. However,
the ἡγεμών is the governor of Thrace, T. Statilius Barbarus, and the ἱερομνήμων
is the eponym of the town, L. Robert, Hellenica, x, 1955, p. 19 n. 1.

[51] Keil and v. Premerstein, Bericht über eine zweite Reise in Lydien, Denkschriften, Akad. Wien, liv, 1911, p. 72 No. 152; restored p. 76 in No. 158;
Quandt, p. 183 f.

[52] Bull. corr. Hell., 1, 1926, p. 242 [Δι]ονύσῳ .... [καὶ συ]μμύσταις ... ις
οἰκέτης δῶρον.

[53] ILS, 3369, *Pontius daduchus spirarches Liberis patris stibadium restituit loco
suo.* 3370, *Achilleus spirarches Liberis patris stibadium restituit loco suo.*

[54] ILS, 3367, *Libero patri spira Ulubrana d. s. p. f.,* from Cora. ILS, 3364,
*Libero patri sacrum T. T. Flavii Eclectianus et Olympianus fil. eius sacerdotes
orgiophantae,* from Puteoli.

[55] ILS, 4061, *Severo et Quintiano cos.* (235 A. D.) *nomina Asianorum. Ger-
manus spirarchaes. Tattario Epipodia mater etc.,* names follow. Mater was in these
times an honorary title.

[56] ILS, 4060, *princ(ipes)* C. Senti, *Verano bul(euta),* T. Ulp. Hr. *sac(erdos)*
C. Va. Valens. *fil(ii)* Valera. et Valentianus, *arc(arius?)* M. Ulp. Iuanus, *frat(er)*
Ulp. Dionysius *lib(rarius) leg(ionis), arc(hi)mys(ta)* Ant. Antoni(us), T.
Ae. Felix *bul(euta), fil(ius)* T. Ae. Antonius, *ecd(icus)* Va. Festus. Many more
names follow.

The titles of the functionaries and members of the Dionysiac associations are the source for our knowledge of the content of these mysteries.[57] There is nothing related to the Oriental religions in them; the Dionysiac mysteries were purely Greek. Unlike the old orgia the Dionysiac mysteries of this age had many functionaries. Some titles were taken over from the old orgia, but these were not sufficient. βάχχαι, βάχχοι are the usual names of the partakers. Iobaccheia was a festival at Athens, mentioned in the speech against Neaera.[58] βασσάρα recurs at Ephesus; it was an old name for a Maenad. A tragedy of Aeschylus has this title. It is said to be derived from a Libyan word signifying "fox". The Iobacchi have an ἀρχίβαχχος and Agrippinilla created male ἀρχιβάσσαροι and female ἀρχιβάσσαραι. Βουκόλοι is a common title, the members of the asscociation in Pergamon being called so. Here there is no need to go into the discussion of the tauromorphic Dionysos who gave them their name, but we may merely note that the Attalids had a certain relation to him.[59] In Pergamon the βουκόλοι were dancers and had a leader, a χορηγός. The ἀρχιβούκολος is often mentioned, by Agrippinilla, in Pergamon, Philadelphia, Abdera, Perinthus, and there is a βουκολικός among the Iobacchi; the special connotation of this last title is not clear. In the inscription of Agrippinilla a large group is called ἀπὸ καταζώσεως and two smaller ones βάχχοι and βάχχαι ἀπὸ καταζώσεως. In an inscription from Philadelphia a κατάζωσμα is a group for which the hierophant and the ἀρχιβούκολος τῆς σπείρης promise to erect an altar to Dionysos Kathegemon.[60] Cumont has discussed the word at length; these people were probably a group distinguished by some special girdle or dress.

---

[57] See the commentary by Cumont in the paper cited p. 46 n. 4, pp. 232 ff., and my remarks in my paper, En marge etc. pp. 9 ff.

[58] Ps. - Demosthenes, lix, 78.

[59] The oracle in Paus., x, 15, 1, ταύροιο διοτρέφεως φίλον υἱόν refers to the victory over the Galatians. Diodorus, xxxiv, 13 and Suidas s. v.ταυρόκερως promise him and his grandson but not his great-grandson the kingdom.

[60] K. Buresch, Aus Lydien, 1898, p. 11 No. 8; Quandt, p. 179 f. ἔτους .... Πα]νήμου λ΄. β[ου]λευσαμένου τοῦ [κατ]αζώσματος βωμ[ὸν] ἀναστῆσαι Καθηγεμόνι Διονύσῳ [Εὐ]τύχης Ἑρμογένου α΄ ἱεροφάντης καὶ Ἕρμ... ος Μενεκράτου α΄ . ος, ἀρχιβούκολος [τῆς σπ]είρης ὑπέσχετο [τῷ κα]τ[αζ]ώσ[μ]ατι.

The old orgia had no hierarchy, but the late age, which loved pomp, created functionaries from the names of implements used in olden times. At Ephesus some members are called θυρσοφόροι, others βουκόλοι and βάσσαραι, and at Attaleia in Phrygia we find a ναρθηκοφόρος; contrary to the proverb: πολλοὶ μὲν ναρθηκοφόροι, παῦροι δέ τε βάκχοι, the ναρθηκοφόρος has become a special functionary. New titles are taken from the mythology. Σειληνοί appear in Pergamon. What the ὑπουργὸς καὶ σειληνόκοσμος mentioned by Agrippinilla had to do is not clear. Cumont's suggestion that, like the εὔκοσμος of the Iobacchi, he had to maintain good order is hardly likely. Much more interesting is the ἄππας Διονύσου at Magnesia ad M.; later on in the same inscription a ὑπότροφος and another ἄππας are mentioned.[61] ἄππας is a nursery word, "papa".[62] He takes care of the child Dionysos, as Silenus does. This interpretation is confirmed by the ὑπότροφος, a subordinate nurse.

The late age which loved and developed a hierarchy had to turn elsewhere as well in order to fill its needs. Of course the associations had priests and priestesses, the Iobacchi even a vice priest, ἀνθιερεύς, for the noble Herodes was too busy to take care of his office. The Dionysiac mysteries borrowed from other mysteries, especially the Eleusinian, which were famous and had great influence on the forms of all other mystery cults. Such borrowing was easy at Ephesus, where the mysteries of Demeter and Dionysos Phleus were united. Here, at Magnesia ad M., at Philadelphia, at Hierocaesarea,[63] at Acmonia in Phrygia,[64] perhaps at Smyrna in the mysteries of Dionysos Breiseus,[65] and in the inscription of Agrippinilla we find a hierophant. In a Latin inscription from Puteoli occurs the word *orgiophantes*,

---

[61] I Magn., 117; Quandt, p. 163; text below p. 65 n. 112.

[62] See Hj. Frisk, Griech. etymologisches Wörterbuch, s. v.

[63] Keil and v. Premerstein, i, p. 54 No. 112; Quandt, p. 181, ἐπὶ ἱεροφάντου Ἀρτεμιδώρου τοῦ Ἀπολλωνίου Μηνόφιλος, Περηλίας καὶ Σεκούνδος Ἀπολλωνίου οἱ συγγενεῖς Διονύσῳ Ἡριχ[ε]π[αίῳ] τὸν βωμόν.

[64] On a small altar, Rev. études anciennes, iii, 1901, p. 276 b; Quandt, p. 211, ἔτους τλα' (246/7 A. D.) σὺν τῇ ἱερᾷ (ει)σ[π]είρῃ ἧς καὶ εἱροφάντης.

[65] CIG, 3210; Quandt, p. 148; see above pp. 47 f.; [ἱεροφαν]τοῦντος is a supplement.

coined after ἱεροφάντης. We come back below p. 138 to the θεοφάντης in Smyrna. In the Eleusinian mysteries a dadouchos came next to the hierophant. In the inscription of Agrippinilla a dadouchos appears; she is a woman and perhaps the word is to be taken literally, "torch-bearer"; the Maenads bore torches. But in an inscription from Rome a man appears as *daduchus spirarches*.[66] New words were invented to designate the leaders: ἀρχιμύστης at Magnesia ad M. and Apollonia, ἀρχιμυστῶν at Perinthus, σπείραρχος in the same place, *spirarches* in Latin inscriptions from Rome and Dacia.

Agrippinilla seems to have had the intention of arranging an imposing procession. A number of persons carrying sacral symbols are mentioned. The λικναφόροι have been mentioned above pp. 45 f. A φαλλοφόρος belongs of course to Dionysiac processions. Others are taken from other cults. The θεοφόροι carried images of gods, a famous instance being the many images of gods, and of the emperor and empress, donated by C. Vibius Salutaris at Ephesus, and carried in processions.[67] πυρφόροι, carriers of fire, are often mentioned, especially in the cult of Apollo. A κισταφόρος appears also at Apollonia and at Thessalonike, and Agrippinilla has three of them.[68] The cista mystica is well known, and is to be seen on Roman monuments representing Bacchic scenes and initiations into the Bacchic mysteries.[69] Pergamene coins of the third century and the first half of the second century B. C. show a cista from which a snake creeps forth; it is Dionysiac, for it is surrounded by a wreath of ivy.

Three functionaries are found mentioned only in the inscription of Agrippinilla, σειγηταί, ἀρχινεανίσκοι, ἀντροφύλακες. Σειγηταί, "the silent ones", are the humblest of the members. Cumont has with probability interpreted their name to mean that silence was imposed upon them during and after the cere-

---

[66] The Latin inscription is cited above p. 54 n. 53.

[67] The latest and complete edition of the inscription in Forschungen in Ephesos, ii, 1912, pp. 127 ff. No. 27.

[68] The inscription from Cyzicus, Bull. corr. hell., xiv, 1890, p. 538 No. 3; Quandt, p. 130 and 265, which mentions κίσταρχοι and μύσται, may refer to mysteries of Kore-Persephone who was the chief goddess of this city.

[69] See below p. 96.

monies. As to the ἀρχινεανίσκοι, he suggests that νεανίσκοι formed a special class of the mystae, though they are not mentioned in the inscription. One may perhaps also think of the *praetor* or *magister iuventutis* who was the head of the *sodalicia iuventutis,* associations common in the Italian cities.[70] We have no certain information about these functionaries.

For the moment we leave the ἀντροφύλακες aside. They bring up another aspect of the Dionysiac mysteries, and we shall come back to them below p. 61. We add a few brief remarks on the functionaries charged with the material interests of the associations. There were not a few among the Iobacchi: the προστάτης is probably to be reckoned among them though we ignore his functions, the ταμίας is the bursar, the γραμματεύς the secretary. The εὔκοσμος of the Iobacchi was a kind of policeman: if someone behaved badly and made trouble, he was to place the thyrsus of the god at the man's side as a token that he must leave. If he did not obey, the ἵπποι, the "horses", were to remove him bodily. The name of these subordinate functionaries is curious: it has been remarked that the Sileni of old vase paintings are half-horses. A ἱερομνήμων is mentioned in the inscription of Agrippinilla, at Perinthus he is the eponym of the town. This is a title of functionaries who took care of the material goods of a god or an association. A διαταξί[αρχος] appears in Pergamon, whose duty it probably was to arrange something, perhaps the ceremonies of the βουκόλοι together with whom he is mentioned. But at Philadelphia the mystae of Dionysos Kathegemon honour an ἐκ τῆς διατάξεως μύστην; this seems to be a special group of the association, as was the κατάζωσμα mentioned above p. 50.

Finally we discuss at some length a few titles which, combined with other information, shed some light on the performances and the character of the Dionysiac mysteries. First the oft mentioned βουκόλοι.[71] The association of Dionysos Kathege-

---

[70] See A. della Corte, Juventus, Athenaeum, xii, 1934, pp. 337 ff.

[71] I relegate to a foot-note some Latin inscriptions in which an *archibuculus dei Liberi* is mentioned, ILS, 1264, 4152, 4153. They belong to the fourth century A. D., in which noblemen were initiated in as many mysteries as possible;

mon in Pergamon was designated by their name. In an inscription οἱ χορεύσαντες βουκόλοι honour a proconsul under whose regime they performed at the biennial festival (τριετηρίς).[72] The inscription goes on to list a διαταξί[αρχος], an ἀρχιβούκολος and other βουκόλοι. The χορεύσαντες βουκόλοι were a selected group. Another inscription honouring an ἀρχιβούκολος[73] lists the names of 17 βουκόλοι, 2 ὑμνοδιδάσκαλοι, and 3 Σειληνοί, and a third, mutilated,[74] preserves mention of οἱ χορεύσα[ντες βουκόλοι] and the ἀρχιβούκολος. Some of the βουκόλοι had to dance, and when a Silenus and the hymn instructors are mentioned together with them we may assume that the Silenus was in some way connected with their performances and that hymns were sung for the occasion. In this age hymns accompanied almost every divine service;[75] in Pergamon the noble college of the ὑμνῳδοί celebrated the emperors. A hymn was sung in the Dionysiac mysteries at Rhodes.[76] In the Orphic hymn book, which probably was collected in Pergamon according to a well-considered plan, hymns to Dionysos hold the central place and are more numerous than those devoted to other gods.[77] Among the Iobacchi the priest Nicomachus had introduced a θεολογία, i. e. sermon.[78]

The office of the βουκόλοι in Pergamon, perhaps elsewhere too,[79] was to dance at the biennial festivals of the god, just as the Maenads did. Even women danced in Asia Minor. The periegete Dionysius[80] mentions Dionysiac choruses of dancing

---

the two last are set up in memory of a taurobolium. ILS, 3269 mentions a *ierof(anta)* and a *spira*: it is uncertain to which cult it belongs.

[72] Athen. Mitt., xxiv, 1899, p. 179 No. 21; Quandt, p. 123.

[73] I Perg., 485; SIG, 1115; Quandt, loc. cit.

[74] I Perg. 486; cf. 486 b; Quandt, p. 128 f.

[75] See my GGR, ii, pp. 360 ff.

[76] See below p. 64 with n. 107.

[77] Cf. my GGR, ii, p. 347.

[78] Loc. cit. ii., p. 362 f.

[79] Scol. Lycophron, v. 212, Δαίμων Ἐνόρχης ὁ Διόνυσος · παρὰ Λεσβίοις..... ἐνόρχης λέγεται διότι μετ' ὀρχήσεως αὐτοῦ ἐπιτελεῖται μυστήρια. The explanation of the epithet rests on a misunderstanding.

[80] Geographi graeci minores, ii, pp. 202 ff., vv. 102 ff.

women at Ephesus. Lucian[81] censures the passion of the people
in Ionia and Pontus for pantomimic dances. The Bacchic dances,
he says, have so enthralled the people there that they sit the
whole day, regardless of all else, watching Titans, Corybants,
Satyrs, and Boukoloi. Even the most high-born and prominent
men take part in these dances without shame, for they rate them
higher than birth and offices and the rank of their ancestors.
These noblemen will not have performed their dances like
common actors in some theatre, they could do it under the
pretext that it was a religious ceremony. These were accomodat-
ed to the taste of the age. A passage in the biography of
Apollonios from Tyana[82] says that in Athens they dance
λυγισμούς, bendings and twistings, and subjects from the epic
poems and the theology of Orpheus, some acting as Horae,
others as Nymphs, and others as Bacchants. It seems that the
dances in the Dionysiac mysteries were no more than an occasion
for performing pantomimic dances, of which the age was
extremely fond. The common idea of Bacchic impersonation
and revelry favoured this propensity.

This being so, it is not surprising to hear that the Dionysiac
technitae, i. e. the professional actors, honoured a man who had
payed for a mystic agon, i. e. in this case theatrical performances.[83] The Bacchic associations sometimes performed sacral plays.
In the statutes of the Iobacchi, lines 120 ff. we read: μερῶν δὲ
γενομένων αἱρέτω ἱερεύς, ἀνθιερεύς, ἀρχίβαχχος, ταμίας, βουκολικός, Διόνυσος, Κόρη, Παλαίμων, ᾿Αφρoδείτη, Πρωτεύρυθ-
μος · τὰ δὲ ὀνόματα αὐτῶν συνκληρούσθω πᾶσι. Comparing
lines 65 ff., which enjoin the members τοὺς μερισμοὺς λέγειν
καὶ ποιεῖν, scholars agree that the members represented the
priests and gods listed, and acted and spoke their parts. Palaimon
had mysteries on the Isthmus,[84] Proteurythmos is mentioned
only here: it may be guessed that he was Orphic or a god of the

---

[81] Lucian, de saltatione, 79.

[82] Philostratus, vita Apoll., iv, 21.

[83] SEG, vi, 59, ἀγωνοτεθῆσαι τὸν ἀγῶνα τὸν μυστικὸν δοθέντα ὑπὸ τοῦ αὐτο-
κράτορος ἐν ὀλίγαις τῇ πόλει, Ancyra; ἀγὼν μυστικός for Dionysos and Demeter
at Side in Pamphylia, Robert, Bull. épigr., 1951 No. 219.

[84] See my GGR, ii, p. 350.

dance; we know nothing for certain. A sadly mutilated inscription from Ephesus is assumed to refer to some such performances.[85] In the introductory words we read θεοῦ Διονύσου and μυστη[ρίων]. The names that follow are so mutilated that it does not pay to enumerate them all, but only to quote those which are tolerably certain: B]ρόμ(ιος), Κόρυνβος, ['A]θηνᾶ Σώτει[ρα] , ['Ο]μόνοι(α), ['A]χελῶ(ος), Κουρῆ(τες), [Ν]ύμφ(αι) πρε(σβύτεραι), [Μ]νεία, "Ηλιος, [Ν]ύμφ(αι) νε(ώτεραι), Κόρη, Πᾶνες, Ἀσκλή-(πιος), [Δ]ημή(τηρ), [Σ]ύγκλ(ητος), νέου Διονύσου θρεπτ(ός) (?). The new Dionysos is the emperor Hadrian, and even the Roman Senate is mentioned. The cult of the emperors was often fused with the mystery cults in Asia Minor. Many names cannot be restored with any certainty. These would seem, however, to be too many for such performances, and the matter must remain uncertain.[86]

The ἀντροφύλακες, "guardians of the grotto", lead us to another side of the Bacchic cult, wine-drinking and the lavish meals. Of course these had a place in many other sacral associations, but in the nature of things they were most prominent in the Bacchic. In the procession of Ptolemy Philadelphos a grotto, covered with ivy and smilax, was carried on a car; two springs gushed forth from it, one of milk and another of wine. Nymphs and Hermes surrounded it.[87] The image of Dionysos himself was placed under a canopy (σκιάς) decorated with ivy, vines and other fruits, and hung with wreaths, fillets, thyrsi, tympana, head-bands (μίτραι), tragic, comic, and satyric masks.[88] The purpose of such artificial grottoes in the cult of Dionysos is made manifest by the account of Mark Antony's visit to Athens.[89] He

---

[85] BMI, 600; the beginning in Quandt, p. 161, the names p. 266.

[86] Cf. Festugière p. 207 n. 2 in the paper cited p. 2 n. 5.

[87] Athen., v, p. 200 C.

[88] Ibid. v, p. 198 D.

[89] Ibid. iv, p. 148 B, quoting Socrates of Rhodes, ἱστορεῖ δὲ καὶ αὐτὸν τὸν Ἀντώνιον ἐν Ἀθήναις μετὰ ταῦτα διατρίψαντα περίοπτον ὑπὲρ τὸ θέατρον κατασκευάσαντα σχεδίαν χλωρᾷ πεπυκασμένην ὕλην, ὥσπερ ἐπὶ τῶν Βακχικῶν ἄντρων γίνεται, ταύτης τύμπανα καὶ νεβρίδας καὶ παντοδαπὰ ἄλλ' ἀθύρματα Διονυσιακὰ ἐξαρτήσαντα μετὰ τῶν φίλων ἐξ ἑωθινοῦ κατακλινόμενον μεθύσκεσθαι. Cf. Plutarch, de sera num. vind., p. 565 F.

constructed above the theatre a scaffold made of fresh wood, such as was used in the Bacchic grottoes, hung from it tympana, fawnskins, and various Dionysiac toys, and got drunk there together with his friends.

Caves were loved because of their coolness in the hot summer and often served as cult places, especially for the Nymphs. According to the myth Dionysos had been nursed by the Nymphs in a cave of Mt. Nysa, and a cave was dedicated to him on Naxos.[90] Moreover, there is an early representation, the archaic cista of Kypselos at Olympia, where Dionysos was depicted in a grotto.[91] On his way back from India Dionysos instituted choruses before a cave at the river Kallichoros in Paphlagonia, and rested in it during the night. According to Oppian, Cynegetica, iv, v. 246, the child Dionysos was concealed in a cave; see below p. 110.

As a matter of course the artificial grotto was decorated with ivy, vines, and other Bacchic attributes. One is reminded of the beautiful kylix of Exekias, showing Dionysos sailing in a boat under the shadow of a big vine with leaves and grapes. The Bacchic grottoes may have been more like the "Laubhütten" that were erected at certain festivals, e. g. the Karneia. They were admirably suited for drinking parties. As to the ἀντροφύλακες of Agrippinilla it is not likely that they carried a grotto; rather they were guardians of the grotto in which the drinking party took place afterwards. A πατὴρ σπηλλέου and ἀρχιμα[γα]ρεύς are mentioned in the inscription from Thessalonike mentioned above p. 53 n. 47; μάγαρον is another name for the Dionysiac grotto.

Since such a grotto could only be used in good and warm weather, generally the Dionysiac associations had a house, a dining hall. In Pergamon a man erected a propylon for a Dionysiac association.[92] As a man at Cyzicus donated a balustrade, a building must be presupposed.[93] At Acmonia in Phrygia the

---

[90] Porphyr., de antro Nympharum, 20; cf. Apollonius Rhodius, ii, v. 910.

[91] Paus., v, 19, 6, Διόνυσος δὲ ἐν ἄντρῳ κατακείμενος, γένεια ἔχων.

[92] I Perg., 297; Quandt, p. 122, ἀνέθηκεν αὐτοῖσι στύλοις πρόπυλον Βρομίῳ Πακοριτῶν.

[93] CIG, ii, 3679; Quandt, p. 130, Αὐξάνων τραπεζίτης τῆς πόλεως καὶ γραμματεὺς τῶν πρώτων βάκχων Κυνοσουρειτῶν τοὺς καγκέλλους ἀνέθηκεν.

first thiasus of the mystae of Dionysos Kathegemon built for themselves an exedra and an adjoining room,[94] probably for their meetings and banquets. At Erythrae the priest of Dionysos built the holy house,[95] but it is not said that he was a priest of a mystery association. But in the remarkable inscription from Magnesia ad M.[96] mention is made of persons who had bequeathed money to the holy house. The house was called Βαχχεῖον at Thasos[97] and probably in a Bulgarian inscription,[98] but at Megara the word signified the association[99] and so too in a Latin inscription from Nicopolis ad Istrum.[100]

The dining couch was called στιβάς, στιβάδειον, Latin *stibadium*. The word occurs so often, especially in the statutes of the Iobacchi, that references are not needed. It signifies originally a bed of straw, rushes, or leaves. This accorded well with the taste for an idyllic, simple, pastoral life that is conspicuous in the Hellenistic age, as well as in the two following centuries. But such a simple bed was not sufficiently comfortable for the luxury-loving people of the age. The name was transferred to permanent constructions with dining couches. So it seems to be in a very mutilated inscription from Pergamon,[101] and when an inscription from Rome[102] says *stibadium restituit loco suo,* the words indicate some construction. Picard has tried to show further that at some places, Thasos, Delos, Pergamon, etc., the *stibadium* was a kind of building or exedra.[103] The associations had of course servants who prepared their meals and served them at their banquets. The inscriptions overlook such people

---

[94] Quandt, p. 211, Διονύσῳ Καθηγεμόνι οἱ μύσται τοῦ ἱεροῦ αʹ θιάσου ἐκ τῶν ἰδίων καθιέρωσαν εἰς τὴν ἑαυτῶν χρῆσιν τήν τε ἐξέδραν καὶ τὸν προσκειμένην δίαιτην.

[95] Bull. corr. hell., iv, 1880, p. 157 No. 4.

[96] τῷ ἱερῷ οἴκῳ τῶν ἐν Κλιδῶνι, quoted in full below p. 65 n. 112.

[97] IG, xii, 8, 387, quoted above p. 51 n. 35.

[98] See above p. 51 n. 36.

[99] IG, vii, 107.

[100] Quoted above p. 54.

[101] I Perg., 222; Quandt, p. 123, Διονύσ[ωι Καθηγεμόνι] καὶ τοῖς [μύσταις or βουκόλοις] Ἀρίσταρχος τ[ὸ σ]τιβάδε[ιον ἀνέθηκεν].

[102] Cited above p. 54 n. 53.

[103] Ch. Picard, Un type méconnu de lieu-saint Dionysiaque: Le *stibadium,* Compte rendu de l'acad. des inscriptions, 1944, pp. 127 ff.

but sometimes members were elected to supervise the banquets. The inscription of the association at Apollonia in Thrace mentions among other functionaries a ἑστία[ρχος], a "maître de cuisine", and a κρατηριακός, a wine steward.[104] A ritual wine-drinking is perhaps indicated in an inscription from Nicopolis in Phrygia ad Hellespontum.[105]

In this respect the Dionysiac mystery associations resemble the other very numerous associations of the Hellenistic and following age, which, under the pretext of honouring some god after whom the association was named, assembled in order to enjoy themselves and to feast. Dionysiac associations, at least that of Dionysos Kathegemon, added the beloved pastime of dancing. Except for this and the hymns, the cult seems hardly more than a pretext for enjoyment. The Iobacchi held meetings every ninth day of the month with wine-drinking, as well as at the ἀμφιετηρίδες, at the Baccheia, and whenever there was an opportune festival of the god. The frequent celebrations are probably the reason why the Iobacchi do not pose as a mystery association, for other Dionysiac associations held to the old tradition of assembling but once a year, as the rule was in sacred festivals, or, in the case of the βουκόλοι at Pergamon, every second year like the Maenads in olden times. The Dionysiac cult had ancient traditions which were not altogether forgotten.

However, it might happen that an association kept more of the content of the Dionysiac religion. There is a hint of this perhaps in the name of the σακηφόροι μύσται at Ephesus.[106] An inscription from Rhodes honouring a priest of Bacchos Dionysos, was mentioned above p. 59.[107] It is a pity that the inscription

---

[104] CIG, 2052, above p. 53 n. 46, perhaps misspelt for κρατηρίαρχος.

[105] Athen. Mitt. xxx, 1905, p. 146; Quandt, p. 129, τὸν Βρομίου μύστην ἱερῶν, ἄρξαντα χοῦ, τὸν καὶ ἐν πατρίδι πάντων ὄντα πρῶτον Φ[λάου]ιον 'Ανδρονεῖκ[ον 'Ο]νήσιμον κτλ.

[106] See above p. 48.

[107] Österr. Jahreshefte, vii, 1904, p. 92; Quandt, p. 204, from the reign of the emperor Caracalla, ll. 23 ff., βακχεῖα, οἷς καὶ ἐφιλοτιμήσατο ἀνδρΟΣΙΝΗ ΙΟΣ * ρ', δόντα δὲ καὶ τῷ ὑδραύλῃ τῷ ἐπεγείροντι τὸν θεὸν * τξ' καὶ τοῖς τὸν θεὸν ὑμνήσασι καὶ [τῇ ἱερεί]α(?)μ', καὶ ταῖς τοῦ θεοῦ δὲ καθόδοις δυσὶ τὸν .... The same festival appears in the inscription, IG, xii: 1, 155; Quandt, p. 203, ἐν τᾶι τῶν Βακχείων ὑποδοχᾶι κατὰ τριετηρίδα.

breaks off precisely at the most interesting point. We should like to know how the awakening of the god and his two ascents were performed. The Lydian inscription mentioning the Orphic god Erikepaios[108] is interesting as showing an Orphic influence. A Pythagorean influence is also apparent if my interpretation of the γαλακτοφόρος is right.[109] The same influences appear in a newly discovered inscription from Smyrna to which we shall return at some length below pp. 133 ff.

Finally we come to a subject of which we shall have more to say when treating the Bacchic mysteries in Italy, namely the care of the dead. In fact there is only one testimony to this from Greek countries, for it is hardly relevant that the last paragraph of the statutes of the Iobacchi prescribes that a wreath worth five denarii shall be sent to the funeral of a deceased member and that the members who attend shall have a wine-drinking. The Iobacchi were not a mystery association and such honours to the deceased were common. Nor is it known if the Dionysiastai at Tanagra who buried a member were a mystery association.[110] The fellow-mystae who built a tomb for a man in Poimanenum in Mysia were perhaps mystae of Dionysos, but this is not stated.[111] More important is an inscription from Magnesia ad M.[112] Here the archimystes reminds the mystae not to forget the persons who have bequeathed money to them for remembrance; accordingly the mystae are to bring the accustomed offerings in the month of Lenaion, from the money left for this

---

[108] See above p. 56 n. 63.

[109] See above p. 53 n. 48.

[110] IG, vii, 686, οὗτον ἔθαψαν τὸ Διωνιουσιαστή.

[111] Athen. Mitt., ix, 1884, p. 35; Quandt, p. 129, Ὑπόμνημα Μενεκράτου τοῦ Ἀνδρονείκου ὃ κατεσκεύασαν αὐτῷ οἱ συνμύσται τῶν [Ποι]μ[αν]ηνῶ[ν].

[112] I Magn. 117; Quandt, p. 163, ἐπὶ στεφανηφόρου Κλ. Ἀπ. Τατιανῆς + Ε-Φιλήτου ὁ ἀρχιμύστης σὺν καὶ Ἑρμέρωτ ... πόρου διεσημειώσαντο πρὸς τὸ τοὺς μύστας μὴ ἀγνοεῖν τοὺς καταλιπόντας αὐτοῖς εἰς μνήμην χρήματα. ὥστε τῷ Ληνεῶνι μηνὶ τὰ εἰθισμένα αὐτοῖς προσφέρεσθαι ὑπὸ τῶν μυστῶν ἐξ ὧν κατέλιπον τῷ ἱερῷ οἴκῳ τῶν ἐν Κλιδῶνι, + μηνύοντες ὁπόσον ἕκαστος αὐτῶν κατέλιπε· Φιλήμων ὁ ἅππας Διονύσου * ιη′ +, Ποσιδώνια ἡ ἱέρια καὶ στεφανηφόρος * κε′ + [Ἀντίο]χος ὁ ἱεροφάντης * ιη′ +Ἐλπὶς ἡ ὑπότροφος * ιε′ + Ἀγαθίας .... ξαγόρας ὁ ἅππας * ιη′ + ἅτινα καὶ ἐκδανείζεται ὑπὸ τῶ[ν μυστῶν]. Beginning of the second century A. D. Cf. above p. 53 and 56.

purpose to the holy house belonging to those at Klidon. It is to be noted that the offerings are to be made in the month of Lenaion, for this was in Ionia the month of the Bacchic orgia.

This is reminiscent of the funeral associations in Rome and Italy, which took care of the funerals and the memorial cult of their members. The spring festival of the Rosalia became, in fact, a festival in memory of the dead, just because the funeral associations chose it for their celebrations.[113] It spread to Thrace and was there sometimes joined with the cult of Dionysos. One inscription indicates a connection with the mystic cult, in another Maenads are mentioned.[114] The relation of Dionysos to the world of the dead was not altogether forgotten in Greek lands.

VI. The Bacchic Mysteries in Italy.

The Bacchic mysteries in Italy are known only through monuments of art. The inscriptions quoted above p. 54 were set up by people of Greek origin and refer to the Greek mysteries. Before we enter upon the difficult task of interpreting the monuments it may be convenient to survey the most important groups.

The most glorious and the best known of all is the great fresco in the Villa Item outside of Pompeii near the Porta Ercolanense. It has often been discussed and I desist from criticizing the earlier attempts of interpretation,[1] submitting my

---

[113] See my paper, Das Rosenfest, reprinted in my Opuscula selecta, i, pp. 311 ff., and my article "Rosalia" in the Realenc. d. class. Altertumswiss.

[114] Bull. corr. hell., xxiv, 1900, p. 305 No. 1, καταλιμπάνω δὲ μύσταις [Δι]-ονύσου δηνάρια ρκ', παρακαύσουσίν μοι ῥόδοις κα[τ' ἔτος]; Ἐφημ. ἀρχαιολ. 1936, παραρτ. p. 17, ἀπέλιπεν τῇ Ὀλδηνῶν κώμῃ δηνάρια ιε' ἵνα ἐκ τοῦ τόκου κρατὴρ γεμισθῇ ἔνπροσθε τῆς ταφῆς καὶ στεφανωθῇ ἡ ταφὴ ἐν ταῖς Μαινάσιν κατ' ἐνιαυτοῦ ἅπαξ; cf. CIL, iii, 703 and 704.

[1] I mention only the most important of these: G. E. Rizzo, Dionysos Mystes, see p. 1 n. 2, with good illustrations of the fresco and kindred monuments;

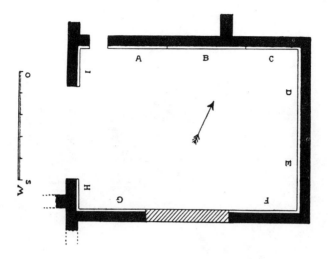

Fig. 9. Plan of the triclinium in the Villa Item.

own to the judgment of the reader. It is the most beautiful and earliest of the pertinent monuments, with large figures painted in the second style, belonging to the last years of the Republic.

The paintings decorate the walls of a great triclinium which has a large window opening on the East portico and two doors, a larger one on one of the small sides and a small one nearby on the left long side. See the plan, Fig. 9. The adjoining cubiculum is also decorated with Bacchic subjects.[2] In the corner at G and H between the great window and the entrance, a dressing

according to him the paintings represent the initiation of the child Dionysos; for criticism see below p. 110. M. Rostovtzeff, Mystic Italy, 1927, pp. 40 ff. with deplorably bad illustrations. "The initiation of a soul into the mysteries is often compared with a wedding, her initiation being thought of as a sacred wedding" (p. 46). M. Bieber, Der Mysteriensaal der Villa Item, Archäol. Jahrbuch, xliii, 1928, pp. 298 f., with good plates. Her opinion that the scenes represent the initiation of brides into the Dionysiac mysteries is taken over with some modification by A. Maiuri in his sumptuous work, La villa dei misteri, 1931, with excellent colour plates in a portofolio. I omit others, Macchiori etc.

[2] Maiuri, loc. cit. pp. 174 ff.

Fig. 10 a.   *The great fresco in the Villa Item, left wall A.*

Fig. 10 b. *The great fresco in the Villa Item, left wall B.*

Fig. 10 c.　*The great fresco in the Villa Item, left wall C.*

Fig. 10 d.   *The great fresco in the Villa Item, rear wall D.*

Fig. 10 e.   *The great fresco in the Villa Item, rear wall E.*

Fig. 10 f. *The great fresco in the Villa Item, right wall F.*

scene is inserted.[3] A richly clad lady sits in an armchair attended
by a servant, an Eros holds up a mirror to her and another Eros
is leaning on a pillar. Nothing warrants the assumption that this
is the dressing of a bride. Erotes are so common in scenes from
the life of women that their presence proves nothing. The sepa-
ration of this scene from the great fresco should be taken into
account, placed as it is in the corner between the large
window and the great entrance door. Between the two doors, at
I in the plan, a stately enthroned lady is seen, and she too is
separated from the great fresco, here by the smaller door.[4] It
may be noted that both these scenes are set upon a higher plan
than that of the great fresco.

These two scenes are clearly separated from the main part
of the fresco, which runs continuously from the small door to
the window opening onto the portico, overlapping the two
inner corners of the room. There is nothing indicating any relation to wedding rites. Behind this opinion lies the thesis of
mystery theology that the neophyte was assured of his eternal
bliss by being united with, wedded to the god; this is unfounded. There is another and more simple explanation of these
two pictures, which are separated from the mystery scenes of the
main part of the fresco, that is that they represent the prepara-
tions, perhaps of the Lady of the House, for partaking in the
celebrations. The so-called mysteries were to many merely great
banquets with a little thrill of religious ceremonies added, just
as in certain modern orders. Naturally, people, especially the
ladies, donned their best attire for such an occasion.

The great fresco is commonly taken to be a representation of
Bacchic mysteries, but this is also contested. In my opinion it is
a mixture of actual rites and mythological material of a kind
that is not rare and is especially frequent in Dionysiac representations; let me recall the mixing of the wine at the Choes[5] and
the vase from Spina.[6] The series of scenes begins from the

---

[3] Rizzo, loc. cit., p. 92, fig. 27; Maiuri, loc. cit., pls. xiii and xiv.

[4] Rizzo, p. 93, fig. 28; Maiuri, pl. xv.

[5] See my GGR, i, p. 555; 2 ed. p. 588.

[6] Described above pp. 24 ff.

small door and continues uninterruptedly to the large opening. There is absolutely nothing mythical in the first two groups. The first centers about a naked boy reading from a papyrus scroll. In the second a seated woman, seen from the back, uncovers with her left hand a tray or dish, brought by another girl, and with her right hand touches another dish in which a girl pours something from a small jug. It is a scene of offering. Then the mythical figures begin. A Silenus is playing on the lyre, a boy blows the double flute, and a girl offers her breast to a kid, below is a goat. It is a pastoral idyll of the kind loved by the Hellenistic age, transposed into the mythical world: the two youngsters seem to be Panisci. A figure follows which is difficult to explain: a woman running away in terror and making an averting gesture. She looks towards her left, but there is nothing terrifying in the following group, the first to the left on the rear wall. There a seated Silenus gives a boy something to drink and another boy helds up a mask over the head of the Silenus; the two boys seem to be Panisci. I think she is terrified by the scene in the corner opposite, the winged woman who is about to flog a young woman. Meanwhile, occupying the center of the rear wall and directly opposite the main entrance, is the scene that is the culminating point of the whole series, the union of Dionysos and Ariadne. Most unhappily the upper part of Ariadne has vanished and the upper parts of two women, standing in the background, are also missing. Before them is a kneeling veiled woman uncovering the liknon. With her the most enigmatical part of the painting begins. Close to the liknon a daemonic female figure is standing, clad in a short cloth around her loins and wearing high boots; she has powerful dark wings. She turns a little to her right but looks to her left, holding in her right hand, which is stretched upward, a long wand with which she seems ready to deal out a blow. She looks and aims at a young woman before her who, clad in a dark cloth but with a naked back, is concealing her head in the lap of a seated woman who lays her left hand on the girl's arm and with the other makes a protecting gesture, looking up at the daemoniacal figure with a terrified and prayerful glance. Lastly there is a dancing, almost completely naked woman clashing cymbals above her

head, and in the background behind her another woman
completely covered by a dark dress, holding a thyrsus and
looking very serious, even sad. The series of scenes comes to
its end at the large window opening on the portico. The most
puzzling and least understood figure is the daemonic woman.
In my opinion she gives the clue to the interpretation, and to
this question we must return below pp 123 ff,

The so-called "Homeric" house at Pompeii has an underground story, containing corridors and rooms. The large and
well-isolated innermost room which seems to have been a
triclinium, and is connected with a kitchen, is the one that
interests us. The decoration of the room consisted originally of
seven scenes with human figures alternating with six representations of sacrificial tables, of which four scenes and three tables
are preserved. Here I note only the two pictures that most concern us. One is a "sacrificial" table:[7] on a base is a basket filled
with fruit, partly covered by a cloth, while from one end a
phallus protrudes; before it stands a cock. For the other pictures
I refer to the lengthy description in Rostovtzeff,[8] and come back
to them later as far as they are relevant to our purpose. The
other is more important, and I come back to it below.[9]

A large house, richly decorated with paintings and stucco
reliefs from the age of the emperor Augustus, was discovered in
the seventies in the garden of a lovely Renaissance villa, the Villa
Farnesina, now the seat of the Accademia dei Lincei. I hope not
to be misunderstood in referring to the ancient building as the
Villa Farnesina. It is described at length by Rostovtzeff,[10] to
whom I refer. The owner of the villa must have been a wealthy
man, interested in the cults and mysteries of Bacchus and even
those of Demeter. A fresco in the corridor is called "Revelation"
by Rostovtzeff; I do not see why. The scene takes place before
a statue of Priapus. Another fresco[12] is called "Sacred instruc-

---

[7] Rostovtzeff, p. 63, pl. viii.
[8] Ibid. p. 77, pl. xiv.
[9] See below pp. 116 and 126.
[10] Rostovtzeff, pp. 114 ff; bibliography p. 171 n. 2.
[11] Ibid., p. 118 and pl. xxii, 2; Rizzo, loc. cit. p. 69, fig. 15.
[12] Rostovtzeff, p. 113 and pl. xxiii.

tion": I am unable to make out details in the reproduction and Rostovtzeff gives no detailed description of this picture, declining also to enter upon an interpretation of the others. We too must leave them aside. More interesting are the stucco bas-reliefs in the corners of the ceiling in room No. 3. One of them, pl. xxiv, 1 in Rostovtzeff, shows a woman displaying a pinax (triptych) to two other women; to me, however, the object seems too large to be a triptych. Another, pl. xxiv, 2, shows a woman holding up a tray with some objects, certainly fruit, among which a phallus rises, and holding an indistinct object (a piece of cloth or perhaps grapes) in her right hand, while at her feet a thyrsus lies on the ground. She descends from a higher plane towards two women, the first holding a garland in her outstretched hands, the other carrying a tray with some indistinct objects on her head and in her right hand probably a jug. Pl. xxv, 1, is fragmentary, but xxv, 2 represents a sacrifice in the presence of a drunken Silenus holding a thyrsus. The stuccoes of room No. 4 are more important. Pl. xxvi, 1 and 2 are important, they will be described below pp. 78 ff. A painting from the corridor of the house is reproduced by Rizzo.[13] We come back to this picture below, p. 81. The very fragmentary Pl. xxvii, 1 is called a Bacchanal, and xxvii, 2 "Revelation of the liknon". A squatting woman is perhaps performing this act, but the liknon is not clearly visible. Before her a Silenus is standing.

Two groups of monuments deserve mention here because they are numerous and often represent Dionysiac scenes. The earliest of these are the so-called Campana reliefs, architectural terracotta plaques with reliefs, belonging to early imperial times.[14] They were made for decorating small temples or luxurious buildings, not for poor people. Two series refer to mysteries, the Eleusinian and the Bacchic, representing various phases of each. A more numerous group of monuments consists of the sarcophagi, representing various subjects from the myths

---

[13] Rizzo, loc. cit. p. 46, fig. 7; our Fig. 13

[14] H. v. Rohden und H. Winnefeld, Die antiken Terrakotten, vol. iv:1, Architektonische römische Tonreliefs der Kaiserzeit, 1911, pp. 52 ff. On the use of these reliefs see the text, p. 45.

and cults of Dionysos. They are later, mainly belonging to the third and fourth centuries A. D.[15] Such sarcophagi were expensive and must have been ordered by well-to-do people. An instance of this is a group of nine sarcophagi, of which seven are now in the Walters Art Gallery in Baltimore,[16] in which members of the noble Roman family of the Calpurnii Pisones were laid to rest. Commonly the sarcophagi represent the Bacchic revel, Dionysos with Ariadne and his cortège, and the triumph of Dionysos. Cult scenes are rare and still rarer scenes referring to the mysteries. These will be discussed below.

Other monuments of various categories sometimes represent scenes pertaining to the Bacchic mysteries. These too will be adduced and discussed below. The numerous representations of Dionysiac subjects and sometimes of Bacchic mysteries prove how popular the Bacchic religion was in Italy and the western provinces.

The monuments teach us something about the particularities of the Bacchic mysteries. Two stucco reliefs in the Villa Farnesina show two stages of the initiation. In the first (Fig. 11) the neophyte stands in the middle, a boy of six or seven years, holding a thyrsus; his head and body are covered by a cloth, and he wears boots. Behind him a woman stretches out her right arm over his head, but unfortunately a piece of the stucco is lost just at this point. Before him is a Silenus uncovering the

---

[15] It is regrettable that the volume comprising the Bacchic sarcophagi in the great corpus initiated by Carl Robert has not appeared. A very poor and incomplete substitute is S. Reinach, Répertoire des reliefs, 1912, of which the third volume comprises Italy. Professor F. Matz is working on this vast undertaking; certainly I shall not live to see it completed. He has published preliminary studies in two papers: Eine bacchische Gruppe, Akad. der Wissenschaften, Mainz, 1952, No. 5, and Der Gott auf dem Elephantenwagen, ibid. No. 10.

[16] K. Lehmann-Hartleben and E. C. Olsen, Dionysiac Sarcophagi in Baltimore, 1942. These sarcophagi, which range from the time of Hadrian to the early third century A. D., were found in two underground burial chambers near the Porta Pia in Rome, certainly part of the private cemetery of the Calpurnii Pisones. Apparently the family was addicted to the Bacchic religion, but the opinion of Lehmann-Hartleben that the form of this religion which they favoured was that of Dionysos-Sabazios is not well founded. On the whole his interpretation is too speculative and not sufficiently factual. Caution is needed.

Fig. 11. *Stucco relief in the Villa Farnesina.*

Fig. 12.   *Stucco relief in the Villa Farnesina.*

Fig. 13. *Painting in the corridor of the Villa Farnesina.*

liknon which stands on a base, the phallus protruding beneath
the covering cloth. To the right is a woman holding a tympanon
in her down-stretched hand and between her and the other
woman a round cista of wickerwork on a base, certainly the
cista mystica. In the second stucco relief (Fig. 12) the same boy
is standing erect, nude, and holding the thyrsus. Before him to
the left a woman stands, but the stucco is here so fragmentary
that her action cannot be made out. To the right behind him
a youth is seated on a rock (?), turning his back to the boy; in
his raised right hand he holds something over the boy's head
(or grasps the branches of a tree). Further to the right a man,
perhaps a Satyr, pours wine into a crater, which stands on a small
base. From the border a thyrsus with fillets projects into the
scene. A picture in the corridor (Fig. 13) shows a very similar
scene. The little boy is standing nude, holding the thyrsus and
wreathed; behind him a woman bends down and stretches out
her arms, taking care of him. Behind her to the right is another
woman holding a tympanon, and to the left before the boy
stands a man.

Fig. 14.   Glass *amphora in Florence.*

Fig. 15. *Marble relief in the Louvre.*

A relief on a small glass amphora in Florence (Fig. 14) again shows a boy, probably of about four years. He is completely nude, only his head is covered by a cloth and he carries on it a liknon; it is covered, but no phallus seems to protrude. Before him to the left a woman is standing; with her right hand she stretches out a leafed branch over the boy's head, and she holds a kantharos in her left hand. To the right behind the boy is a thymiaterion, then a small figure of the bearded Dionysos with a thyrsus on a high base, and further a big Silenus-mask on a base.

On a marble relief of debased workmanship in the Louvre (Fig. 15) the little boy appears again. He is nude and carries on his head a tray filled with fruit; from behind a bearded man helps him, before him is an altar with some offerings. On the altar an object stands, similar to a house-shaped lantern used to protect a flame. To the right of the altar stands a woman who seems to be laying something down on it; she has a rich head-dress and holds in her left hand what is probably a thyrsus, though it looks more like a scepter. Behind the altar a large curtain is suspended between two trees that frame the scene, and behind the curtain a column rises, of which only the Corinthian capital is visible. Something stands on the capital which Rizzo calls a triptych; it is, however, too large. It resembles a small naiskos, but it is empty. This relief represents a sacrifice, not an initiation.

A painting from Nero's Domus Aurea, which is preserved only in a drawing[17] (Fig. 16), occasions some doubts. Two women are holding up a tray or large basket with a low rim above a small figure, who is clad in boots and wears a large cloak that covers his head. The figure looks like an adult but may be a child. On the tray is a big cone surrounded by a wreath to which long fillets are bound; it is not a phallus. To the left is a group of two women, to the right a man, wreathed and holding a thyrsus, emerges from the knees up and to the right of him a woman likewise emerges from the hips up. She raises the lid of a cista. It seems that common elements can be recognized, but they are distorted. One cannot rely on the old sketch.

A gladiator helmet found at Pompeii, on which both sides of the crest are adorned with scenes of the Bacchic cult and mysteries, is a sign of their popularity. I reproduce new illustrations after photographs (Figs. 17 a and b), but as even in these details are difficult to discern I repeat Rostovtzeff's description.[18] Four scenes of Bacchic ritual are seen on each side. "The central is again a scene of initiation very similar to that represented on the Louvre bas-relief and reproduced above [our fig. 15]. An old Silenus is represented putting the sacred liknon on the head of a naked boy who is to carry the liknon to a priestess seated or standing near the altar. The priestess seems about to lift the veil which covers the phallus of the liknon. The group of the Silenus and the naked boy is identical with that of the Louvre bas-relief, while the figure of the priestess is different. To the left of this group a scene of Dionysiac ecstasis is represented, a Maenad dancing in the presence of the Silenus. Below, a repetition of the scene with the sacrificial animal on the other side

---

[17] By Francesco de Hollanda in the codex Escurialensis.

[18] Rostovtzeff, Mystic Italy, pl. xx, p. 95; the descriptions pp. 96 and 94.

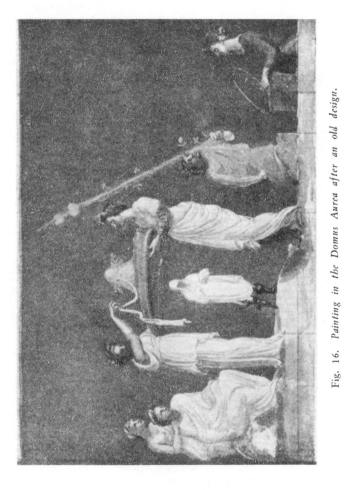

Fig. 16. Painting in the Domus Aurea after an old design.

Fig. 17 b. *Gladiatorhelmet from Pompeii, left side.*

of the crest. Finally, to the right of the central scene, another
curious ritual Dionysiac scene is shown. Three Satyrs are busy
around a large circular kettle. One is kindling a fire (?) under
the kettle. Two others are holding a pig over the kettle in such
a way that its genitalia above the kettle."

"The central scene" of the other side (Fig. 17 b) "curiously
enough is an exact repetition of one of the designs which appears
on the 'Campana' bas-reliefs in terracotta [our Fig. 18]. The
scene represents the initiation of a mysta and the revelation to
the initiated of the phallus. To the left of this scene is a rustic
sanctuary of Dionysos under a beautiful tree, the centre of the
sanctuary being occupied by a statue of Dionysos. Between this
and the central scene is a sacrificial table. To the right of the
central scene is the representation of a ritual act which is figured many times on similar monuments, for example on the
Thraco-Mithraic icones .... From a sacrificial animal (probably
a pig or a sheep), suspended by its hind legs to a tree, the entrails are being removed and the blood collected in a large dish.
The last scene (in a second register below) represents a sacrifice
to Priapus."

The Campana relief mentioned here (Fig. 18) is interesting
because it shows the initiation of an adult man. Behind him to
the right is a woman with a tympanon. The man is covered,
head and all, by a large cloak. A woman grasps his head with
both hands and bends him down. She looks at a Silenus who is
bringing the liknon with fruit and the phallus. It is uncovered
and the cover hangs from his left hand, with which the Silenus
carries the liknon.

A sarcophagus in the Villa Medici (Fig. 19) provides an interesting representation of a Bacchic initiation. The central figure
is a half-nude woman who holds a scroll before her; in front of
her is a jar with fruits (?) and behind her the gable of a temple
is seen. The person who is to be initiated is covered by a great
mantle, but the face is visible; she (it seems to be a woman) is
leaning forwards and is led by a man carrying a thyrsus, whose
head is lost. To the left of the central figure is a seated woman
who holds up a plate of fruit in her left hand; she stretches her
right hand backwards and holds a branch or stick with which

Fig. 18. *A Campana relief.*

she stirs the contents of a big krater in which another woman is pouring something from a jug. Behind this group is a man who carries a veiled liknon on his head; the phallus rises beneath the cover. A small temple is seen behind the left-most group. At the far right is a half-nude woman leaning on a herm with a bearded head, while in the background the head of a bearded man is seen. The following scenes, Pan sitting on a rock and Dionysos finding Ariadne, are not reproduced here.

Another sarcophagus, also in the Villa Medici, may be added, although it does not represent an initiation but a sacrifice, for it shows the close similarity between these two acts. The pictures (Figs. 20 a and b) make a lengthy description superfluous. To the left is a table on which a crater is standing, a woman puts something on it which resembles a liknon. Then follows a woman with a torch in her hand and carrying a liknon on her head, further another woman pouring out a libation on a heap of fruits placed on a low altar. To the right is a sacrificial scene, similar to those seen on the gladiator helmet (p. 88) and on one of the Arretine cups (pp. 93 ffff.). A man holds up a sacrificed animal and another takes out its entrails.

Fig. 19. *Sarcophagus in the Villa Medici, Bacchic initiation.*

Fig. 20 a. *Sarcophagus in the Villa Medici, Bacchic sacrifice.*

Fig. 20 b. Sarcophagus in the Villa Medici, continued.

I append a discussion of two Arretine cups, both by Perennius, similar but not identical: one is in the Museum at Arezzo,[19] the other in New York.[20] Many individual figures are identical but they are arranged in different order.[21] I begin with that in Arezzo of which Rizzo has published a design (Fig. 21). In the middle towards the left is a group. A woman lays down a garland on an altar, behind it rises a column with a small image of Priapus on its top. On the other side of the altar a seated Satyr plays the double flute and treads a κρούπεζα. Towards the right a woman follows, carrying a liknon on her head and holding a jug in her down-stretched right hand. The next figure is a Satyr holding up a small torch in his right hand and carrying on his back a sack, perhaps a wine-skin. The following group represents a sacrifice: a woman and a Satyr hold up a pig, he stabs it with a knife in the throat, and the blood streams down into a basin. Behind him there is a column with an amphora on its top. On the other side of this a bearded, bald-headed Silenus carries a baby. Then, above the drape of a large curtain, appear the head and hands of a woman, clapping casta-nets. The altar scene follows.

To describe the cup in New York we begin with the sacrificial scene (Fig. 22 b). To the left is the column with the amphora, to the right the woman carrying the liknon, in which the phallus is plainly visible. Here too (Fig. 22 a) the sack-carrier follows her, but before him comes the Silenus carrying the baby and then the column with the amphora and the curtain with the castanet player behind it. The altar scene seems to be missing. The photos reproduced by Cumont do not present exactly each a

---

[19] Rizzo, loc. cit., figs. 1 and 2, p. 41.

[20] G. H. Chase, The Loeb Collection of Arretine Pottery, 1908, p. 41 and pl. I, reproduced by Cumont p. 240, figs. 1 and 2 in the paper cited p. 46 n. 4.

[21] This is explained by the technique which H. Dragendorff, Terra sigillata, Bonner Jahrbücher, xcvi-xcvii, 1895, p. 55, describes: The potters had separate convex stamps, exactly modelled in clay, of each element of the decoration, figural as well as ornamental. These stamps were impressed in the inner side of a mould so that it had all the figures and ornaments on its inside. This was fired and then the vessels were moulded in it. Thus the figures and the orna-ments could be arranged at will.

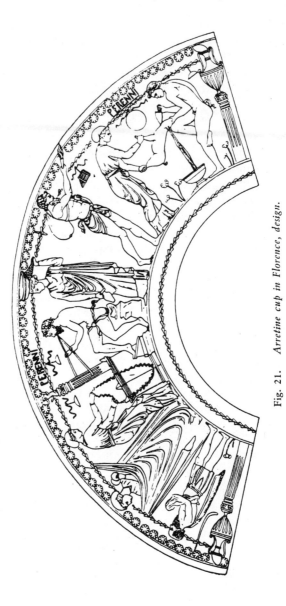

Fig. 21.   Arretine cup in Florence, design.

Fig. 22 a and b.   *Arretine cup in New York.*

half-part of the cup, for the right margin of Fig. 22 b overlaps a
little the left margin of Fig. 22 a. Thus a gap is left between the
right margin of Fig. 22 a and the left of Fig. 22 b, but it is too
small for the fairly large altar scene.

Rizzo hails the baby as the child Dionysos. I do not see the
reason. The child Dionysos was carried to the Nysaean nymphs,
and we shall have more to say of this very popular representation
below pp. 111 ff. More probably the scene represents a human
baby being consecrated to Dionysos. Below in our ch. vii we shall
see that even very small babies were initiated into the Bacchic
mysteries, "consecrated to Dionysos" would be a more proper
expression. The liknon-bearing woman refers clearly to the
Bacchic mysteries. As usual the representation is transferred onto
the mythical plane, with Satyrs and Silenus appearing instead
of men.

This survey lets us know the elements of the Bacchic mysteries
and more of the same kind will be added by other monuments
to be noted below. The liknon, the sign of the Bacchic mysteries,
appears everywhere. It is carried on the head of a woman, or in
the hands of a Silenus, or on the veiled head of the neophyte, or
is held above his head. Even the culminating point, the revela-

Fig. 23. *Part of mosaic from Cuicul (the whole Fig. 31).*

tion of the phallus, is seen on the stucco relief from the Villa
Farnesina (Fig. 11). Other monuments represent this act much
more conspicuouly, e. g. the fresco in the Villa Item (Fig. 10 e)
and the mosaic from Cuicul (Fig. 23).

The cista mystica was in this age a common symbol of the
mysteries, and the Bacchic mysteries also employed it. It is seen
on Fig. 11 and sometimes on sarcophagi.[22] The paraphernalia
of the old orgia were regarded as characteristic of the Bacchic
cult in general, and appear everywhere: the thyrsus, the tympana
in the hands of women, even castanets. In this age Dionysos was
principally the god of wine. Women hold kantharoi in their
hands, wine is mixed in big craters (Fig. 12 and 19), and if my
interpretation is right a Satyr carries a wine-skin on his back
(Fig. 21 and 22). Wine miracles are recorded from this age.

———

[22] E. g. on two sarcophagi in Baltimore (see p. 78 n. 16) representing the
childhood of Dionysos, and Dionysos and Ariadne. S. Reinach, Répertoire de
reliefs, iii, p. 326, 5; p. 361, 1; p. 435, 3.

According to Diodorus the inhabitants of Teos claimed that at a certain fixed time, viz. a festival, a fountain of wine streamed forth in their town. The same tale is told of the island of Andros; the miracle was repeated every second year at a festival called Theodaesia, probably the old festival of the Maenads, the Lenaea. At the festival of the Thyia in Elis three empty vessels were brought into a room and its door was sealed; the next day they were found full of wine. In a temple in Corinth an apparatus has been found that is supposed to have served for a wine miracle.[23]

An animal sacrifice is represented on the gladiator helmet from Pompeii (Fig. 17 a) and on the sarcophagus in the Villa Medici described p. 89 (Fig. 20 b), but it is a separate scene not connected with the scene representing the initiation. And though on the Arretine cups a sacrifice appears as an integral part of the decoration, the technique of these vases makes it doubtful if this scene belonged originally to the Bacchic mysteries. If, as probably happened commonly, the Bacchic mysteries were celebrated indoors, an animal sacrifice was less appropriate, offerings of fruits much more so. This must must be the intention when fruit are carried not in a liknon, but on a tray or in an ordinary basket. Thus the relief in the Louvre (Fig. 15) does not represent an initiation but an offering of fruit, a very common scene. They were the more appropriate because the liknon itself contained fruit.

A few words must be added on the masks which sometimes appear on monuments related to the Bacchic mysteries. In the group to the left of Dionysos and Ariadne on the fresco of the Villa Item a Satyr boy holds up a Silenus mask above the head of a Silenus. The initiation scene on the glass amphora in Florence (Fig. 14) shows to the right a big Silenus mask on a base which is draped by a cloth. A relief at Verona shows a liknon filled with fruit and over it, but seemingly not attached to it, a big mask, more like that of a Satyr than of Dionysos.[24] On a picture from

---

[23] References in my GGR, i, pp. 556 f., 2nd ed. pp. 589 f. with notes.

[24] Th. Schreiber, Hellenistische Reliefs, pl. 101; J. E. Harrison, Journal of Hellenic Studies, xxiii, 1903, p. 318, fig. 14.

Fig. 24. *A child's sarcophagus from Carthage.*

the house of the Vettii at Pompeii a mask leans against the
upper end of the liknon.[25] On the relief in Vienna (Fig. 7) three
masks, one tragic, one comic, and one satyric, together with a
lyre surround the pillar on which the liknon is placed. A child's
sarcophagus from Carthage (Fig. 24)[26] is peculiar. A child has
donned a Silenus mask, much too big for him, two children before
him seem to be afraid of the sight, and behind him are two
others of whom the foremost carries a jug in his hand.

The mask was from of old the symbol of Dionysos.[27] Then it
became especially appropriate to him as the god of the theatre.
It may be objected that the masks were added merely because
they were paraphernalia of Dionysos. However, the picture in
the Villa Item, the initiation scene on the glass amphora in
Florence, and likewise the relief in Vienna and the picture in
the House of the Vettii seem to prove that the mask had a proper role in the Bacchic mysteries, and the sarcophagus from
Carthage may also be understood in this sense. It is certainly
not impossible that it was used in some way in the initiations
into the Bacchic mysteries.

---

[25] Monumenti antichi, vii, 1898, p. 310, fig. 33.

[26] S. Reinach, Répertoire des reliefs, ii, p. 3, 3.

[27] W. Wrede, Der Maskengott, Athen. Mitt., liii, 1928, pp. 66 ff.

Appendix

on a Relief in the Carl Milles Collection

There is an unpublished relief in the Carl Milles collection
at Lindingö near Stockholm (Fig. 25) which may be of some interest for the Bacchic mysteries. I owe the photograph and an
exact description to Dr A. Andrén, sometime keeper of this collection.[1] "A marble plaque, breadth 35.5 cm., height 46 cm. The
main figure has naked feet and is clad in a chiton reaching down
to the feet with half-length sleeves; over this he wears a hide which
is fastened on the left shoulder and round the waist a broad
girdle; the head and the forepaws hang down on the breast. His
hair and beard are stylized in archaic fashion, long, spiral-form
locks hang down on the back and the shoulders and shorter ones
on the forehead; around the head is a diadem. The lowered left
hand holds a cluster of grapes, the right a horn from which a
libation is poured on the altar before him. The altar is square
and profiled at the top and the bottom and decorated with a
garland. A heap of round fruits is laid on the top of it and on
this the head of a goat with long, curved horns, striated transver-
sally.[2] At the corner of the altar stands the base of a much smaller

---

[1] Cf. his Guide to the Collection of Ancient Sculptures, Stockholm 1952,
No. 74.

[2] Zancani Montuoro (quoted below p. 103, n. 13) explains the curved object,
seen on the burning altar on some vase pictures (her figs. 6, 7 and 9), which generally
is taken to be the tail of the sacrificed animal, as a goat's horn. The Keraton at
Delos and the altar at Dreros prove that special attention was paid to goats' horns
at the sacrifice, but, as far as I know, they were not nailed up like the bucrania.
The goat was the animal commonly sacrificed to Dionysos. A goat's head is seen
on the altar on the left side of the Ariadne sarcophagus in Baltimore, and on the
right side of the Triumph sarcophagus it is placed between two griffins; see
Lehmann-Hartleben etc. fig. 13 and 5 resp. (cited above p. 78 n. 16). The aetiolo-
gical explanation was that the goat injured the vines by nibbling at them. So they
do on a black-figured vase, figured in my GGR, i, pl. 49, 4. See the story of the
origin of the askoliasmos, Verg., Georg., ii, vv. 380 ff.; Hygin., Astron., ii, 4,
probably from Eratosthenes' Erigone. In an epigram of Leonidas from Tarentum

Fig. 25.   *Relief in the Carl Milles Collection.*

figure of Priapus. The lower part of the figure is formed as a
tapering square pillar or herm without feet, the upper part as a

the vine replies to the goat which nibbles at it that in spite of this the roots will
produce enough wine to suffice for pouring out a libation over it when it is
sacrificed; Anthol. pal., ix, 99; cf. 75 by Euenos from Ascalon. More in Roscher,
Lex. d. Mythologie, i, p. 1038. That the goats were a real nuisance to the vines
is shown by an inscription treated by L. Robert, Hellenica, vii, p. 153.

naked man, ithyphallic and with a bearded head; it wears a
head-gear similar to a tutulus and on the shoulders a hide or
mantle which hangs down over the arms and is knotted on the
breast. The figure holds in its raised right hand a cornucopia
and in the lowered left hand an object which on close consi-
deration is not to be taken for a *pedum*[3] but for a gardener's
knife of the type which is seen e. g. on the Antinoos relief[4] and
on two reliefs in the Vatican, representing shops where knives
are made or sold.[5] Similar knives are still used in Italy today.
Behind Dionysos (or his priest) is a palm tree and behind the
figure of Priapus a tree of another kind. The phallus of Priapus
is broken off, so also a bit of the left arm of the main figure;
this part is, however, stuck on again with gypsum. Traces of the
drill in the fruits, the garland, the cornucopia, the tree, and the
grape cluster, as well as the archaic type of Dionysos seem to
date the relief in the second century A. D."

At first glance one would say that Dionysos is represented
sacrificing to Priapus, but there are very serious objections to
such an interpretation. Miss Simon has given the title "Opfernde
Götter" to an interesting book;[6] it is misleading, for it suggests
a god offering a sacrifice to some other god. In fact such a god
is never represented; the gods of the vase paintings which she
treats pour out libations, holding a phiale in their hands. They
are not comparable to our relief. The book ought to have been
called "Spendende Götter in der attischen Vasenmalerei". Two
examples seem to be more relevant, showing other sacrificial
implements than the phialae. A Hellenistic relief represents
Artemis Eupraxis, carrying a sacrificial basket and kindling the
fire on the altar with a torch,[7] but here too there is no god who
receives the sacrifice. The worshippers, a man and two women,

---

[3] As I have done in my Guide, l. c. (Andrén).

[4] Ducati, L'arte in Roma dalle origini al secolo VIII, Tav. cxxxvii (Andrén).

[5] U. E. Paoli, Das Leben im alten Rom, pl. lix (Andrén).

[6] Erika Simon, Opfernde Götter, 1953. See also B. Eckstein-Wolf, Zur Dar-
stellung spendender Götter, Mitt. d. deutschen archäol. Instituts, v, 1952, p.
39 ff.

[7] Figured in Arch. Jahrb., xl, 1925, p. 211, fig. 1.

stand before the altar, the man seems to lay down something on the altar. A bronze relief of the same age from Delos is similar.[8] The goddess, Artemis, holds two torches and lowers that in her right hand to kindle the fire on the altar. On its other side a Satyr, bending down, seems to place a billet on the altar and to blow the fire. To the left behind the goddess is another Satyr carrying a jug in his right hand and a liknon on his head. Its contents are very difficult to discern. Courby took them to be a sacrificial animal, a dog, but Vallois, who has scrutinized the original, contests this. He says p. 249: *En avant, " une boule informe", à droite de laquelle on distingue une petite feuille trilobée, puis deux tiges à extrémités barbelées, qui semblent sortir de la même gaine, enfin un objet vertical, dont le relief a été usé, et qui se termine par de longs traits parallèles un peu inclinés"*. That is, the liknon is used for carrying offerings. In the background to the right is a very small idol standing on a high and slender small pillar with a square capital; it is clad in a dress reaching down to the feet and holds in the outstretched hand seemingly a torch. She is called Hekate, but the long robe does not suit Hekate, nor Artemis. The interpretation of the goddess is dubious; here only the sacrificial scene is of importance. Both these reliefs show the goddess Artemis, whose attribute the torch was in this age, kindling the fire on the altar, not performing a sacrifice: she looks away from the idol. The sacrifice is made by the Satyrs. The interpretation is that the goddess receives the sacrifice by purveying the sacrificial fire.[9] The vase painting which shows Themis with a sacrificial basket and a torch before Bendis is allegorical: it is right to venerate the newly introduced goddess Bendis.[10] That a god should

---

[8] Published by F. Courby, Monuments Piot, xviii, pp. 19 ff. pl. vi; Brunn-Bruckmann, Denkmäler, pl. 621; discussed at length by R. Vallois, Bull. corr. hell., xlv, 1921, pp. 242 ff. with fig. 2.

[9] The coin from Enna, reproduced in Farnell, Cults of the Greek States, iii, Coin plate No. 4, does not belong here; it shows a goddess holding a torch upright at the side of an altar.

[10] V. Ehrenberg, Die Rechtsidee im frühen Griechentum, 1921, pl. to p. 32; better C. Watzinger, Griesch. Vasen in Tübingen, 1924, pl. 40. Cp. my GGR, i, p. 71 n. 1, 2nd ed. p. 80 n. 6.

sacrifice to another god implies a contradiction. The Greeks felt so. When Alexander the Great offered to the Ephesians to dedicate the temple of Artemis, they answered that it was not becoming for a god to make offerings to another god.[11] If then it is impossible to take the said representations as sacrifices in the common sense of offerings brought to a god, another explanation must be found. In certain cases the representations are similar to a libation at a farewell or a banquet, but this is not sufficient explanation for the scenes adduced. Vase paintings sometimes represent statues of gods with phialae in their hands.[12] It cannot be meant that the statues are pouring out libations. Likewise a cup or a kantharos is the common attribute of the gods on the votive tablets from Locri in South Italy. The gods are standing or seated, sometimes a sacrifice is brought to them.[13] They cannot possibly be sacrificing or pouring out libations. One is reminded of the words of Aristophanes that when we pray to the gods for something good their statues stand stretching out an upturned hand, not to give anything but to get something.[14] I think that the most common act by which veneration was paid to a god was transferred to the representations of the gods themselves in order to show their divine nature. The god's attitude is, so to speak, a projection of the worshipper's attitude.

The idea of the great god Dionysos sacrificing to Priapus seems to me to be really too strange to be accepted. If this seemingly obvious interpretation is rejected it must needs be supposed that the majestic figure is the priest who has donned the attire

---

[11] Strabo, xiv, p. 641. It does not matter if the anecdote is historical or not, it shows what the Greeks thought.

[12] A vase picture recently published by E. Bielefeld, Zur griech. Vasenmalerei des 6. bis 4. Jahdts, 1952, pl. xxvii, shows a xoanon between two thymiateria holding a phiale in each hand.

[13] See e. g. the tablet published by Paola Zancani Montuoro, Tabella fittile locrese con scena del culto, Rivista del R. Instituto d'archeologia e storia dell' arte, vii, 1940, pp. 206 ff., pl. i (reconstruction), figs. 2 and 4. More in Q. Quagliati, Rilievi votivi arcaici in terracotta di Lokroi Epizephyrioi, Ausonia iii, 1908, pp. 136 ff., figs. 29, 31, 32, 33, 47, 56.

[14] Aristophanes, Eccles. vv. 780 ff.

of the god. We remember that in certain Bacchic associations members appeared in the roles of certain gods; even Dionysos himself is mentioned among these in the statutes of the Iobacchi. There are a few instances in which a woman appears in the attire of a goddess in a procession;[15] they are hardly comparable. In the mysteries at Pheneos the priest put on the mask of Demeter Kidaria and beat the ἐπιχθονίους with a stick.[16] Only this example is really relevant and belongs probably to the Hellenistic age.

I know only one monument comparable to the relief in the Carl Milles collection, a relief on a round base, formerly in the Lansdowne collection (Fig. 26).[17] The attitude and the dress of Dionysos are almost identical, but on the Lansdowne relief he holds a kantharos from which he pours out a libation on the altar and he wears boots with upturned toes, while on our relief he is barefooted. The altar too is very similar, but it seems that a burnt sacrifice is being offered. Four round objects, resting directly on the surface of the altar, seem to be the ends of billets; what rests on these is indistinct, but a flame seems to be rising from it. Behind the altar there is no Priapus, a Maenad comes immediately before the god. Especially important is that Dionysos is surrounded by three ecstatically dancing Maenads.[18] They are taken from a series of eight Maenads of which certain are well known. Rizzo advances the opinion that the original composition, representing the eight Maenads and Dionysos as the

---

[15] Artemis at Patrae and Delphi, Paus., vii, 18, 12; Heliodorus, Aethiopica, iii, 4; Athena at Pellene, Polyaenus, Strateg., viii, 59, a doubtful anecdote. Cp. F. Back, De Graecorum caerimoniis in quibus homines deorum vice funguntur, Diss. Berlin 1883.

[16] Paus. viii, 15, 3: πρόσωπον.

[17] It is published by G. E. Rizzo, Thiasos, bassirelievi greci di soggetto dionisiaco, 1934. This is a sumptuous publication, privately printed in only 250 copies. I owe a copy to the zeal of Mr G. Filipetto, Secretary of our Institute in Rome, and the kindness of the Dottoressa Maria Santangelo. The figure of Dionysos is again reproduced by J. Marcadé, Trouvailles de la maison dite de l'Hermès, Bull. de corresp. hellénique, lxvii, 1953, p. 508, fig. 12. The base is now in the collection of Lady C. M. Whittall at Haslemere.

[18] Rizzo, l. c., figures 10, 11, and 13, pp. 20, 21, and 23 resp.

Fig. 26. *Relief on a base, formerly in the Lansdowne Collection.*

central figure, was due to the sculptor Kallimachos, ὁ κατατηξί-
τεχνος, who lived in the latter part of the fifth century B. C.,
and Marcadé agrees with him. The sculptor, who in the second
century A. D. made the relief in the Carl Milles collection,
changed his model to suit the Dionysiac cult of his time. He
separated the god from his Maenads and added a Priapus to

whom the sacrifice is made. This being so, colour seems to be lent to the opinion that not the god himself is meant but his priest, who in this age sometimes donned the attire of Dionysos.

VII. The Child in the Bacchic Mysteries.

The child holds a principal place in the representations of the Bacchic cult, mysteries, and myths in this age. A child is the neophyte in all the initiation scenes reviewed above except two. Children are often seen among the Satyrs and Maenads who follow Dionysos in the representations of his myths on the sarcophagi. Drunken and happy children swarm on the sarcophagi, e. g. on one in the Lateran[1]; they replace the thiasus of Dionysos. At the left end Pan and a dancing Maenad are seen, at the right there is a statue of the bearded Dionysos, while a woman offers fruit in a basket. Another sarcophagus from Ostia[2] shows on the main side children drinking and making music. This is continued on the two small sides, while the fourth shows children boxing and wrestling.

Exceptionally we have one passage in the literature referring to the initiation of babies into the Dionysiac mysteries.[3] It is late, from about the middle of the fourth century A. D. The rhetor Himerius had lost his son Rufinus, when he was a child at his mother's breast, and wrote a commemorative speech on him. He says that the child had let its locks grow for Dionysos and asks Dionysos why he ravished the boy from his sanctuary; now the boy has been initiated in the sanctuary below without having his father as mystagogue, a gloomy Bacchic feast; and finally he asks how he can trust in Dionysos who did not save the boy. Apparently, the child was not yet initiated, but it had been intended that he should be very soon.

---

[1] F. Cumont, Symbolisme funéraire, pl. xl, 2; cf. p. 344.

[2] Ibid., p. 471, figs. 101 and 102.

[3] Himerius, oratio xxiii; the words quoted are found in §§ 7, 8, 18. See also the inscription cited p. 49 n. 21.

Fig. 27. *Relief in Bologna.*

Another testimony is a relief in Bologna,[4] said to have come from Alexandria (Fig. 27). It is of bad workmanship, probably belonging to the third century A. D. A boy is reposing on a couch; he holds a thyrsus in his left arm and a kantharos in his right hand. The inscription informs us that he died at the age of three years and two months. The attributes show the belief that he partook of the happy Bacchic afterlife, and the reason for this was certainly that he had been initiated into the Bacchic mysteries.

How were children initiated into the Bacchic mysteries or, better, consecrated to Dionysos, when they were too small to take any part in the ceremonies themselves? The monuments give the answer. The cups of Perennius have been described above pp. 93 f. The liknon-bearer proves that the representation refers to the Bacchic mysteries. Into their assembly a bald-headed Silenus

---

[4] Published by K. Schauenburg, Archäol. Jahrbuch, lxviii, 1953, p. 69, fig. 23.

Fig. 28.   *Small side of a sarcophagus*
at Cambridge.

carries a baby in his hands. The baby will be consecrated to
Dionysos, or, we may say, initiated into the Bacchic mysteries.
This is a very simple act, but it seems to be made more im-
pressive if I understand some representations rightly. One of the
small ends of a sarcophagus in the Fitzwilliam Museum at
Cambridge (Fig. 28)[5] shows a bearded man and a young man,
both with torches, carrying between them a liknon in which a
child is seated. There is nothing mythical about the men. The
scene is however, as so often, transferred into the mythical
sphere on a sarcophagus at Naples; here the child is carried by
Satyrs.[6] This is also the case on a Campana relief showing a
Maenad brandishing a torch and a Satyr a thyrsus; both dance
ecstatically and hold between them a liknon from which dra-
pery, vine leaves, and grapes hang down, and in which a child
is seated.[7] (Fig. 29).

---

[5] J. E. Harrison, Prolegomena to the Study of Greek Religion, p. 525, fig.
152. The whole sarcophagus in S. Reinach, Répertoire de reliefs ii, p. 443. The
other small end shows Pan reposing before a curtain, and before him two
children. The main side represents the Indian triumph of Dionysos.

[6] I know it only through the mention in Harrison, loc. cit. p. 524 n. 4.

[7] A. Baumeister, Denkmäler des klass. Altertums, ii, pl. xviii, fig. 932; British
Museum, Catalogue of the Terracottas, D 525, pl. 41; v. Rohden und Winnefeld,
loc. cit. pl. xcix.

Fig. 29. *A Campana relief.*

It is not difficult to understand why children were consecrated to Dionysos — or initiated into the Bacchic mysteries — by
being put into a liknon and swung in it. I do not think it sound
to appeal for a prototype to Dionysos Liknites. This epithet is
in fact very rare in Greece and it was certainly not known to the
Roman public, except for learned men like Servius. In Asia
Minor and the Greek countries we hear nothing of the initiation of children, except for Himerius in the fourth century
A. D. But the liknon had become the characteristic symbol of
the Bacchic mysteries, and it was also used as a cradle for babies.
The idea lay near at hand of placing the baby in a liknon and
thus to consecrate it to Dionysos.

Children were not initiated into the old mysteries[8], nor into the Oriental mysteries. The initiation of children into the Bacchic mysteries is in fact an exception that requires explanation.

Rizzo has advanced the opinion that the child who is seen being initiated on the monuments is Dionysos himself, and because of this he has given the title "Dionysos Mystes" to his tract. That Dionysos is initiated into his own mysteries would imply a contradiction: Dionysiac mysteries would exist before Dionysos himself. Of course this would seem to be the case in the long quotation from Nonnos[9] which is Rizzo's chief argument. He might also have quoted Oppian, who has a long description of the childhood of Dionysos, including the institution of his mysteries.[10] The prototype is apparent, the myth of the childhood of Zeus, which has been adapted to that of Dionysos. Nonnos has done it more skilfully by introducing the nymph Mystis who, while caring for the child, institutes the mysteries. But these late authors do not afford proof that such an idea was current three centuries earlier. Like Himerius they may have known the initiation of children into the Dionysiac mysteries and embellished their description of Dionysos' childhood with new features. The child Dionysos may have been considered as a prototype of the human child initiate, no more, and so others too may have envisaged the initiated child. The initial fact is the admission of children to initiation into the Dionysiac mysteries.

---

[8] The role of the παῖδες ἀφ' ἑστίας μυηθέντες, boys or girls belonging to noble, especially Eleusinian, families, is unexplained. The inscription, IG, i², 6, better SEG, x, 6, lines 106 ff., prescribes that nobody shall be initiated without paying dues, except τὸ ἀφ' ἑ[στίας μυομέν]ο

[9] Nonnos, Dionysiaca, ix, vv. 111 ff.

[10] Oppian, Cynegetica, iv, vv. 244 ff., Ino, Antinoe, and Agaue take care of the new-born child and

εἰλατινῇ χηλῷ δῖον γένος ἐγκατέθεντο,
νεβρίσι δ' ἀμφεβάλοντο καὶ ἐστέψαντο κορύμβοις,
ἐν σπέι καὶ περὶ παῖδα τὸ μυστικὸν ὠρχήσαντο,
τύμπανα δ' ἐκτύπεον καὶ κύμβαλα χερσὶ κρόταινον
παιδὸς κλαυθμυρμῶν προκαλύμματα· πρῶτα δ' ἔφαινον
ὄργια κευθομένη περὶ λάρνακι κτλ.

The background is the sentimental love of children, which begins in the Hellenistic age and persists in the following centuries.[11] It appears very markedly in the many putti swarming on the Bacchic sarcophagi and in the winged boys and small girls with butterfly wings, called Erotes and Psychae, who busy themselves with the jobs of adults, e. g. in the paintings of the house of the Vettii. The admission of small children to the Bacchic mysteries is in a certain measure comparable to their admission to the drinking festival of the Choes in old Athens, but there cannot be any connexion between these two customs, although the Attic custom survived into the Roman age.[12]

As we have said, the increasing love of children provides the background, but no more; there must be a special reason why children were admitted to the Bacchic mysteries. This is clear to see, for the childhood of Dionysos is very prominent in his myths, and no other god is comparable with him is this respect, not even Zeus. I do not mean the Orphic myth that the child Dionysos was lured by the Titans, dismembered, and restored to life again by Zeus. This crude myth was certainly repellent to the easy-going public that favoured the Bacchic mysteries. It is another myth of Dionysos' childhood that was popular precisely in the same age as his mysteries, his education by the Nysaean nymphs. The name Νύσαι is old, found already on a vase of Sophilos of the early sixth century B. C.,[13] and the subject recurs on a beautiful crater from Spina, dated to the

---

[11] Cf. C. Schneider, Die griechischen Grundlagen der hellenistischen Religionsgeschichte, Archiv f. Religionswissenschaft, xxxvi, 1939, pp. 300 ff., the chapter: Verweiblichung und Verkindlichung, pp. 317 ff.; H. Herter, Das Kind im Zeitalter des Hellenismus, Bonner Jahrbücher, cxxxii, 1927, pp. 250 ff.; Th. Birt, Woher stammen die Amoretten? in his book: Aus dem Leben der Antike, 1918, pp. 134 ff.

[12] See the inscription of the Iobacchi, line 130 and the epitaph, IG, ii², 13139/42, ἡλικίης χοικῶν, ὁ δὲ δαί[μων] ἔφθασε τοὺς χοῦς, with a relief representing a nude boy about three years old. Cf. Philostratus, Heroic., xiii, 4.

[13] See my GGR, i, p. 533, 2 ed. p. 567. In regard to the Attic vases of the fifth and fourth centuries see H. Metzger, Les représentations dans la céramique attique du IVᵉ siècle (Bibl. des écoles françaises, vol. 172), pp. 21, 106 ff., 392.

second quarter of the fifth century B. C. (Fig. 30).[14] A nymph holds out the child, who has a twig of ivy in his right hand and a crater in his left. He turns toward a bearded and laurel-wreathed god holding a sceptre, Zeus. To the left of this group is a nymph with a small panther and to the right another, holding flowers. A beautiful representation exists on a silver alabastron of the fourth century B. C., found in Thessaly.[15] A nymph is seated on a rock, the boy stands on her knee, and another nymph stretches her hand out toward him. A thyrsus leaning against a tree and a tympanon suspended in it show what is meant.

These examples may suffice for classical times. In the age and in the countries in which the Bacchic mysteries flourished the examples are so numerous that only some few can be selected.[16] The reliefs of the sarcophagus in Munich show the child bathed, swaddled, and played with. That in the Villa Albani, which is, in fact, the sarcophagus of a child, shows it bathed, played with, and riding on a goat. A third in the Walters Art Gallery in Baltimore shows the child bathed and swaddled, and adds the Bacchic revel.

A full description must be given of a very beautiful mosaic, discovered at Cuicul in Algeria and dated not later than the beginning of the third century A. D., because it is almost a

---

[14] S. Aurigemma, Il Museo di Spina, 2nd ed., 1936, pl. lxxxi and p. 170. Another crater of the same date, pls. lxxxiv and lxxxv, p. 178, is an enigmatic representation. The bearded Dionysos sits on a throne (it must be he and not Zeus, as Aurigemma says, for he holds a thyrsus and the seat is spread with a fawnskin). On his knee a little figure is standing, wreathed with ivy and holding a drinking cup in his right hand and a branch in his left; it is probably a branch of a vine, though it has no leaves. Rostovtzeff, who has used this group as the frontispiece of his book, identifies the figures as the Indian Bacchus and the Eleusinian Iacchos, but Iacchos is never represented thus. It seems to be the child Dionysos, but then the god is doubled. Perhaps a servant?

[15] Athen. Mitt., xxxvii, 1912, pp. 76 ff., pls. ii and iii.

[16] Rizzo, loc. cit., p. 43, fig. 3, reproduces a sarcophagus in the Capitoline Museum, and p. 44, fig. 5, another from the Glyptothek in Munich, and a fresco in the Villa Farnesina, p. 45, fig. 6. In S. Reinach, Répertoire des reliefs, I have noted these sarcophagi: ii, p. 74, 3 in the Villa Albani; iii, p. 59, 3, in Milano; p. 136, 1, a fragment p. 183, 6 in Munich.

Fig. 30.   *Red-figured crater from the necropolis at Spina.*

Fig. 31. *Mosaic from Cuicul.*

repertory of scenes related to the Bacchic mysteries.[17] But the middle field is alien to the cycle if it does not hint at the punishment of the enemies of Dionysos: a man aims with a double axe at a recumbent woman almost naked; she is inter-

[17] L. Leschi, Mosaïque à scènes Dionysiaques de Djemila-Cuicul (Algérie), Monuments Piot, xxxv, 1935—36, pp. 139 ff. and pls. viii and ix.

preted as the nymph Ambrosia killed by Lykourgos. The four side fields present a cycle of the Dionysiac subjects dear to the mystae. The first field shows to the left a woman holding a naked child, Dionysos, in her lap, to the right a half-reclining Satyr into whose mouth wine pours down from a drinking-horn, and in the middle another woman. The second field shows the child Dionysos, helped by a woman, riding on a tigress led by a Satyr. The third is a scene of sacrifice performed by an elderly man; the interpretation referring to the gift of wine to Ikarios seems doubtful, it may be a common sacrifice. The fourth field finally has a scene referred to above p. 96. To the left a kneeling woman reveals a large phallus, grasping it with her hand, in a liknon which stands before her; to the right is a seated woman, holding a cista in her lap, in the middle a woman in a long robe, turning away and with both hands making an averting gesture (see below pp. 128 f.). Leschi says that a trace of a wing is seen at her right shoulder, but it is hardly perceptible and must have been very small; the other shoulder is irreparably damaged. The scene is the same as that on the Campana reliefs and the cameos. Leschi suggests tentatively the name of Psyche for the woman; this is improbable. The room seems to have been a triclinium, for according to information in a letter of M. Leglay the channels beneath the floor were filled with ceramic and glass ware.

The admission of children to the Bacchic mysteries was exceptional. It was conditioned by the myth of the childhood of Dionysos, reared by the Nysaean nymphs, and the sentimental love of children, prevalent in the age when these mysteries flourished, and which well-to-do parents were able to indulge. If they lost a child of tender years, this could be a comfort to them, they would be sure that the child was enjoying a happy afterlife in the company of the god. We come back to the afterlife in our next chapter. But this practice shows also that the Bacchic mysteries were not mysteries in the strict sense of the word, they were not hidden in secrecy.

VIII. The Afterlife.

The old mysteries had no written texts. Such texts appear for the first time in the foreign cult of Sabazios, which was introduced into Athens in the fourth century B. C.[1] Aeschines read from books when his mother performed initiations. When new mysteries were created and old ones remodelled in the Hellenistic age texts were needed.[2] Through the edict of Ptolemy Philopator, who ordered that the holy writings should be brought to Alexandria (above p. 11), we know that the Dionysiac mysteries in Egypt had sacred books. The figure next to the first on the great fresco in the Villa Item is a boy, naked except for boots, reciting something from a papyrus scroll. A seated woman places her arm around his neck as she looks down attentively at him and at his scroll; she too has a scroll in her other hand. It is no mere chance that this group occupies the first place in the series of scenes. On the sarcophagus in the Villa Medici, described p. 88, representing an initiation, the central figure holds a scroll before her.

A wall painting in the "Homeric" house at Pompeii[3] is of great interest. I repeat Rostovtzeff's description condensed. A half-naked girl is seated on a four-legged seat in a thoughtful attitude; before her is a large crater and to the right a shield. Behind her stands a veiled woman with her right hand lifted. Both look at a naked boy who holds before him a large tablet. Between the boy and the two women there is, slightly in the background, a winged woman with a palm-branch in her left hand and a key[4] in her right hand. She is gazing with deep atten-

---

[1] Demosthenes, de corona, xviii, 259, μητρὶ τελούσῃ τὰς βίβλους ἀνεγίγνωσκες; cp. de falsa legatione, xix, 199.

[2] Cf. my GGR, ii, p. 91.

[3] Rostovtzeff, loc. cit. p. 78 with pl. xiv; cf. p. 54. The painting is faded, some details cannot be discerned even in the new reproduction, given here.

[4] Rostovtzeff says p. 78 "a little hammer or key-like instrument". It cannot be a hammer, but a key. The correct explanation is given by Mr Zeph Stewart in a letter to the author: she is the Dike κληδοῦχος of Parmenides. See below p. 125 n. 25.

Fig. 32.   *Wall painting in the "Homeric" house at Pompeii.*

tion at the tablet displayed by the boy. We come back to the interpretation below p. 126, for the winged woman gives perhaps a clue to the contents.

The ever increasing concern of the age with the afterlife, its happiness or terrors, has put its stamp on the Bacchic mysteries too. Before we quote the decisive testimonies and analyze the monuments, some words are needed on the relation of Dionysos to the Nether World. He was not originally a god of the Dead, and though he came to be so regarded, this is limited to certain places. No traces are found of such a belief in Attica in the classical age. This is the conclusion which may be drawn from two learned papers treating the Chthonic Dionysos in vase painting.[5] The god with whom Dionysos is assimilated or identified is Plutos-Pluton, and this god is not to be simply equated with Hades, the Lord of the Dead. The etymology shows who Pluton was originally, the god of wealth, an underground god, but not a god of the dead. On the vase paintings he carries the cornucopia, which is not an attribute of the Lord of the Dead. The name Pluton was not added to the Lord of the Dead until the fifth century B. C.;[6] Pluton-Hades is a euphemism like Eumenides-Erinyes. Metzger concludes rightly that Dionysos was not received into the Eleusinian mysteries until the beginning of the fourth century B. C. In Central Greece and South Italy Dionysos was clearly related to the dead in the classical age.

A series of terracotta protomae found in Boeotia and Locris and belonging to the fifth and fourth centuries B. C. are of great interest for the relation of Dionysos to the dead.[7] Some of them represent him holding an egg in the left hand and a kantharos in the right, in others he has only the kantharos, not the egg. Others, and they are more common, represent a female

---

[5] H. Metzger, Dionysos chthonien d'après les monuments figurés de la période classique, Bull. corr. hellénique, lxviii-lxix, 1944—45, pp. 296 ff., especially pp. 314 ff.; K. Schauenburg, Pluton und Dionysos, Archäolog. Jahrbuch, lxviii, 1953, pp. 38 ff.

[6] See my GGR, i, p. 422, 2nd ed. p. 471 f.

[7] See F. Winter, Die Typen der figürlichen Terrakotten, i, p. 248, figs. 3—5; the much more numerous female protomae, pp. 247—250. A good copy in the National Museum in Copenhagen is reproduced here (Fig. 33).

Fig. 33. *Boeotian terracotta in the National Museum in Copenhagen.*

divinity who has various attributes, a cock[8] in the left hand

[8] The cock appears often on tomb monuments, but also in erotic scenes, see L. Couve, Ephemeris archaiologike, 1897, p. 69; G. Weicker, Athenische Mitteilungen, xxx, 1905, pp. 207 ff. According to Porphyrius, de abstinentia, iv, 16,

and, at least in one copy, an egg in the right. These representations raise a question of great importance, but very controversial and difficult. We have seen that the Bacchic mysteries treated here were created in the Hellenistic age and took over from the old orgia titles of the officials, some paraphernalia, and the mythical apparatus, and from the Dionysiac processions notably the phallus; but their relation to the dead and the World of the Dead is not accounted for, since Rohde's view that the belief in immortality had its origin in the cult of Dionysos cannot be maintained. Numerous terracottas found at Tarentum and Locri show that there Demeter and Persephone were chthonian goddesses and that Dionysos was associated with them in a chthonian aspect. And we have the famous inscription from the first half of the fifth century B. C. from Cumae forbidding those not initiated into the Bacchic mysteries to be buried in a certain place. In Southern Italy Dionysos was a god of the dead in the sixth and fifth centuries B.C. A Faliscan skyphos at Heidelberg[9] from about 370/60 B.C. shows Bacchic revelry in the presence of Pluto in his beneficent aspect. Pluto is enthroned, white-haired, holding a cornucopia; behind him Hermes on a low base, before him a satyr with a tympanon and a crane; on the back side a dancing maenad and a dancing satyr with a tympanon and a panther fell. In the fourth century B.C. and the beginning of the third numerous funerary vases painted with scenes from the Underworld were produced in South Italy.[10] The magnificent great amphoras belong to the latter part of the fourth century. In the middle there is often a building in which the gods of the Underworld are enthroned. They are surrounded by figures drawn from common myths: Tantalos, Sisyphos, Megara and

---

it was sacred to Demeter as a chthonian goddess. The cock and the egg are often seen on the Locrian terracottas; see Q. Quagliati, Rilievi votivi arcaici di Lokroi Epizephyrioi, Ausonia, iii, 1908, pp. 136 ff.

[9] Published by K. Schauenburg, Arch. Jahrb., lxviii, 1953, pp. 38 ff. with figs. 1 and 2.

[10] A collection of these vases is found in Wiener Vorlegeblätter, Ser. E; two are reproduced in Baumeister, Denkmäler des klassischen Alterums, iii, pp. 1927 ff. The Canosa vase, Wiener Vorl., pl. i; Baumeister, pl. lxxxvii; the Altamura vase, pl. ii and fig. 2042 A resp. A new find see p. 125. Cf. my GGR, i, pp. 776 f., 2nd ed. pp. 824 f., with further literature.

her sons, the Danaids, Heracles with Kerberos, Theseus and Peirithoos watched by a woman with a drawn sword. The presence of the judges of the Dead proves that the thought of rewards or punishments in the Other Life was felt intensely, and punishment is dealt out by female daemons: they are called Ποιναί, Punishers, on the Altamura vase. Orpheus playing on his lyre is almost omnipresent, but Eurydice does not appear. The painter had in mind not the visit of Orpheus to the Under-world to fetch his wife, but most probably Orpheus' teaching about the afterlife, especially punishments and rewards. This suggests that these paintings may have been inspired by the Orphic poems, called Κατάβασις εἰς Ἅιδου, which contained old myths, but also added Orphic material.[11] Orphism was from of old widely spread in Sicily and South Italy; many of the alleged authors of Orphic writings are said to belong to this part of the Greek world. Dionysos does not appear on these vases, but they show how prominent the belief in the Underworld was in these regions, and in the same regions the chthonian aspect of Diony-sos was most prominent. A bare century later the Bacchanalia were severely repressed by the edict of the Roman Senate in 186 B.C. It is supposed that they came from Tarentum, but it is very difficult to discern the actual facts in the romanticized account in Livy. There is no hint of any relation to the belief in the afterlife. So much is probably correct, that they were a deteriorated and extravagant form of Bacchic mysteries.

Dionysos' relation to the Underworld and Orphism had old roots in South Italy and in regard to what has been set forth above one may be tempted to suppose that the Bacchic mysteries of the Roman age originated there. But they have other aspects too than the belief in the afterlife and they were widely spread also in Greece and Asia Minor. In Asia Minor they had a special character owing to the fact that mysteries sometimes were grafted onto old cults of Dionysos, and also to the love of the inhabitants

---

[11] See Kern, Orphicorum fragmenta, 293—296, pp. 304 et seqq. The Nekyia in the eleventh book of the Odyssey has been said to be Orphic. It is not so, but it has certainly been a model of the Orphic poems, which drew largely on earlier literature.

for dances and pantomimes. Plutarch gives the most valuable information concerning the mysteries in Greece; some mysteries celebrated the descent of Dionysos to the Underworld. His relations to the Underworld were older; the Boeotian terracottas show that he was a god of the dead in the fifth century B.C. There was probably some variation in different countries and places. Owing to the scarcity of our information we cannot say whether there was a marked difference between Greece and Italy. It may be that the mysteries were levelled and simplified in Italy according to the taste of the Roman public. It seems that these Bacchic mysteries originated in various places but drew on common stock: the old orgia, the familiar myths, and Orphism. They were common and spread almost everywhere like the so-called Orphic gold-leaves.[12]

It may be added that some few inscriptions prove that Dionysiac associations cared for the burial and the cult of their deceased members at Cumae, Tanagra, and Magnesia ad M., and that the Roman funeral festival of the Rosalia in Thrace was combined with Dionysiac elements.[13] The inscriptions from Thrace and Asia Minor are so late in date that Roman influence cannot be excluded, and in regard to the Rosalia it is in fact certain.

Two literary passages which have been unduly neglected state that the belief in the punishments and horrors of the Underworld were integral elements of the Bacchic mysteries.

In his polemic against the Christians Celsus compared them to those who introduced the apparitions and horrors in the Bacchic mysteries.[14] Plutarch alludes to the gloomy aspect of the Other Life in his letter of consolation to his wife, written at the loss of a small daughter. He says: "I know that the words

---

[12] I have not taken these up because their content is different, they do not refer to Dionysos. See my Gesch. d. griech. Religion, ii, pp. 223 ff. A new copy has been found in a tomb dated in the middle of the fourth century B.C. near Pharsalus, Ephemeris archaiologike, 1950—51, pp. 80 ff.; Revue des études grecques, lxv, 1952, pp. 152 f. They are found in Thessaly, Crete, South Italy, and Rome, and their time ranges from the fourth century B.C. to the second A.D.

[13] See above pp. 65 f.

[14] Origenes, contra Celsum, iv, 10 διόπερ ἐξομοιοῖ ἡμᾶς τοῖς ἐν ταῖς Βακχικαῖς τελεταῖς τὰ φάσματα καὶ τὰ δείματα παρεισάγουσι. Cf. viii, 48.

inherited from our ancestors and the mystic symbols of the Dionysiac mysteries which we both know, and of which we partake, prevent you from believing that nothing bad or painful can happen to those who have passed away."[15] The important fact is that in Plutarch's time the Bacchic mysteries had symbols referring to an afterlife corresponding to the deeds of the deceased.

Having this fact in mind we will try to see if anything in the monuments alludes to these beliefs. The most enigmatical figure in the great fresco of the Villa Item is the daemonic woman. (Fig. 10 e, p. 72). If she can be explained the key of the riddle is found, but the many and various explanations proposed, that she is Iris, Adrasteia, Nemesis, Erinys, Aidos, Telete, or Ὁσία, are neither satisfactory nor convincing. I shall not waste space criticizing them. Scourging is known from some few Greek cults, but they do not help, especially since it has been proved that the interpretation of the scourging of the Spartan boys as conferring luck and fertility is erroneous. The attire of the daemonic woman is remarkable, the short loin cloth and the high boots. A short dress and high boots are worn by huntresses and on South Italian vases by punishing daemons, Ποιναί[16]. Like those the woman is a punitive daemon. Such were known in the Bacchic mysteries of the Roman age. The interpreters have overlooked the words of Celsus quoted by Origenes who says that Celsus compared the Christians, viz. their belief in the punishments of Hell, with those who introduced the apparitions

---

[15] Plutarch, Consol. ad uxorem, p. 611 D, καὶ μὴν ἃ τῶν ἄλλων ἀκούεις, οἳ πείθουσι πολλοὺς λέγοντες ὡς οὐδὲν οὐδαμῇ τῷ διαλυθέντι κακὸν οὐδὲ λυπηρὸν ἔστιν, οἶδ' ὅτι κωλύει σε πιστεύειν ὁ πάτριος λόγος καὶ τὰ μυστικὰ σύμβολα τῶν περὶ τὸν Διόνυσον ὀργιασμῶν, ἃ σύνισμεν ἀλλήλοις οἱ κοινωνοῦντες. These seem to be strange words in a letter of consolation, they must be understood in their context. Plutarch begins by saying that little Timoxena was content with little. The sentence quoted follows. He goes on to say that the soul is imperishable and if it lives for a long time in a body is soiled by the contact with it and is invested anew (in a body). Little Timoxena who died at a tender age was free from such a stain, he means, and will have a happy afterlife. These are Plutarch's own speculations. Metempsychosis was probably foreign to Bacchic ideas of afterlife although Orphism knew it.

[16] Inscription on the Altamura vase; see p. 121.

and horrors in the Bacchic mysteries.[17] The daemonic woman is just such a terrific apparition. If I were asked to give her a name I should suggest Dike, Justice. Sophocles says that Dike dwells with the gods of the Underworld.[18] She is mentioned more than once in the Orphic literature. She is said to be a daughter of Law and Piety.[19] A passage in the first speech against Aristogeiton, which has been inserted among the speeches of Demosthenes but belongs to Hellenistic times, is especially relevant. The speaker turns to the inexorable, august Dike, of whom Orpheus, who has taught the most holy mysteries, says that she is enthroned at the side of Zeus and supervises everything among men.[20] Proklos says explicitly that Dike judges souls.[21] This testimony is very late, from the end of Antiquity, but if you consider that the Orphics demanded a moral life and that they taught that men's fates were different in the Other Life, then a judgment after death of the deeds of men in their life was needed. The idea of such a judgment is much older than Plato, in whom the three judges appear for the first time. Pindar speaks of Necessity as a judge, Aeschylus of Hades or another Zeus, i. e. Zeus in the Underworld.[22] The Orphics who spoke so much of Dike made her a judge of the dead, a most appropriate function. The wording shows that they took her from Hesiod whom they used much.[23] The woman who with

---

[17] Cited above, p. 122 n. 14.

[18] Soph. Antig., v. 451, ἡ ξύνοικος τῶν κάτω θεῶν Δίκη.

[19] Hermias in Plat. Phaedrum, p. 248 C = Kern, Orphicorum fragm., 105, ἡ μὲν ἐκεῖ (viz. in the cave of Nyx) Δίκη θυγατὴρ λέγεται τοῦ Νόμου τοῦ ἐκεῖ καὶ Εὐσεβείας; cf. fragm. 159; 160; 181.

[20] Pseudo-Demosthenes, xxv, 11 = Kern, Orphicorum fragm. 23, τὴν ἀπαραί-τητον καὶ σεμνὴν Δίκην, ἣν ὁ τὰς ἁγιωτάτας ἡμῖν τελετὰς καταδείξας Ὀρφεὺς παρὰ τὸν τοῦ Διὸς θρόνον φησὶ καθημένην πάντα τὰ τῶν ἀνθρώπων ἐφορᾶν Cf. Hymn. Orph., lxii.

[21] Proklos in Plat. rempubl., ii, p. 145, 1 Kroll, = Kern, Orphic. Fragm., 158, ὁ Ὀρφεύς φησιν· τῷ (Διί) δὲ Δίκη πολύποινος ἐφέσπετο πᾶσιν ἀρωγός εἰ γὰρ πᾶσιν ἀρωγὸς πολύποινος, εἰ τῷ δημιουργῷ τοῦ παντὸς συνδιακοσμεῖ τὰ πάντα, θεῶν ἄρχει. δαίμοσι συνεπιστατεῖ, ψυχὰς διαδικάζει καὶ ἁπαξαπλῶς διὰ πασῶν διέρχεται τῶν ψυχῶν ἡ κρίσις.

[22] See my GGR, i, p. 775, 2nd ed. p. 823 f.

[23] Hesiod, Opera, v. 259 et seqq.

drawn sword watches Theseus and Peirithoos on South Italian vases is inscribed Dike.[24] Dike is rarely represented in art, but she appears as a winged goddess on a South Italian vase, of which large sherds with scenes from the Underworld were found at Ruvo.[25] The names of the figures are inscribed. In the middle is Persephone enthroned in a temple from which Vekata (Hekate) proceeds; to the left is Orpheus playing on his lyre; seated to the left Δίκη, above her a winged figure in a long robe opening a door, Δίκα. They are the Dike who acquits and the Dike who condemns, the latter is disappearing. Another South Italian amphora shows a scene of punishment in the Underworld. To the left is a judge, who carries a scepter with an eagle, similar to the one on the Altamura vase; then the goddess of the Underworld, and to the right an ugly winged female daemon clad in a loin cloth and high boots fettering a criminal. Another whose hands are tied behind his back is lying on the ground.[26] She may be called Ποίνη, and the same name may perhaps fit the daemonic woman on the fresco in the Villa Item. The name is less important, it is the function of the daemonic figure that matters.[27]

There are finally (Fig. 10 f.) the two contrasting figures, the naked dancing girl and the serious looking woman in a dark robe, carrying a thyrsus, in the background. I do not think that the

---

[24] On a fragment of an amphora at Karlsruhe, Wiener Vorlegeblätter, Ser. E, pl. vi, 3; cf. the Canosa vase. See A. Winkler, Die Darstellungen der Unterwelt auf unteritalischen Vasen, Breslauer philologische Abhandlungen, iii:5, 1888, pp. 12 and 36.

[25] M. Jatta, Monumenti antichi, xvi, pp. 517 ff. and pl. iii. The letters above the winged figure which Jatta took to be ΔΙΚΑ are rightly read ΔΙΚΑ by A. Dieterich, Archiv f. Religionswissenschaft, xi, 1908, p. 159. He points out that Dike is the door-keeper in Parmenides, fragm. 1, v. 14 Diels, τῶν δὲ Δίκη πολύποινος ἔχει κληῖδας ἀμοίβους. It is supposed that these verses are of Orphic origin; cf. Kern, Orphicorum fragmenta, 158.

[26] Wiener Vorlegeblätter, Ser. E. pl. vi, 4.

[27] Some scholars come near to a similar interpretation. Kern in Pauly-Wissowa's Realencycl. d. klass. Altertumswissenschaft, s. v. 'Mysterien' p. 1312, calls her a kind of Erinys. Rizzo, loc. cit., p. 87, sees also a similarity to the Erinys and adds that the punishing and avenging daemons culminate in the Orphic Ananke and Adrasteia. They speak only in terms of a general probability.

naked dancing girl is a member of the assembly,[28] she symbolizes
the joyful aspect of the Bacchic afterlife.[29] The contrast between
her and the dark-robed serious woman is hardly a mere artistic
device; she reminds us of the idea of the gloomy side of afterlife,
and therefore she recedes into the background.

In the light of this interpretation the painting in the "Homeric" house at Pompeii, described above p. 116 (Fig. 99), will
be better understood. Two women look attentively at a boy who
holds a tablet before him. In the background the winged woman
appears, holding a palm-branch in her left hand and a key in
her right. As Mr Stewart explains, she is the Dike κληδοῦχος
who acquits or condemns.[30] The palm-branch in her hand is the
sign of victory, of admission to a happy life in the Other World.

Another painting in the same house seems suggestive (Fig. 34).[31]
An old man seated on a chair is speaking seriously to two women;
one of them is stately and looks attentively at him; she holds the
hand of a veiled girl standing behind her; to the right is Charon
in his boat. Rostovtzeff locates the scene in the Underworld and
interprets the two women as Mnemosyne and a soul. I wonder
if it is not more reasonable to interpret the scene thus, that the
man gives instruction to a neophyte who is protected by a woman
already initiated, and to see in Charon a hint at the contents of
the instruction;[32] they concern the Afterlife, perhaps not exclud-
ing its horrors.

---

[28] Unless she is hired. Such a one is certainly the naked dancing girl at a
banquet on a stele from Mysia; see my GGR, ii, pl. 14, 3 and p. 639.

[29] A striking instance is a tomb monument in the museum of Arlon: within
a curtained recess stand two men and two women, probably two brothers and
their wives, at the sides are a naked dancing Bacchant clapping the castanets and
a Satyr holding up a bunch of grapes. Similar small naked figures adorn the
panels of the angle pilasters. Excellently reproduced in Mrs A. Strong, Apotheosis
and Afterlife, pls. xxv and xxvi, pp. 200 ff.

[30] See above p. 116 n. 4.

[31] Rostovtzeff, Mystic Italy, pp. 68 and fig. x.

[32] A similar symbolic intrusion of Charon in a scene of real life is seen on a
white lekythos; Charon in his boat is put at the side of the tomb monument, on
the other side a woman with offerings is standing, W. Riezler, Weissgrundige
attische Lekythen, pl. 89; Rostovtzeff, l. c. fig. xi.

Fig. 34.   *Wall painting in the "Homeric" house of Pompeii.*

Fig. 35. *A Campana relief, fleeing Dike.*

The winged daemonic woman is one of the apparitions and terrifying figures that were introduced in the Bacchic mysteries, reminiscent of the evil fate awaiting the unjust in the afterlife. But salvation is at hand. Close to the left of the winged woman the girl reveals the liknon with its contents, promising life and luck. The following act is represented on some Campana reliefs[33] (Fig. 35), on two cameos[34] (Fig. 36), and on a mosaic. On the Campana reliefs a young man is to the left, then the kneeling girl revealing the liknon, to the right a winged woman running away hurriedly. The girl takes hold of a corner of her long robe to hold her back, but she makes an averting gesture. The cameos are similar. Instead of the youth there is a Silenus holding up a basket of fruit,[35] and the object revealed is a bearded bald head,

---

[33] v. Rohden-Winnefeld, iv:1, p. 52, fig. 98, pl. 123; Rizzo, Dionysos Mystes, fig. 21, p. 81.

[34] Bieber, loc. cit., p. 309, fig. 8; Journal of Roman Studies, iii, 1913, p. 163, figs. 29 and 30; Rizzo, l. c., fig. 23 b, p. 83.

[35] Cf. p. 97.

Fig. 36.   *Cameo in the Bibl. Nat. Paris*

probably that of a Silenus; before the winged woman is an altar. The dress of the winged figure is different from that of the figure from the Villa Item: on the reliefs she has a long flowing robe, on the cameos it is shorter, reaching to the knees. In spite of this difference the three winged women represent certainly the same figure, Dike.

The same motif seems to be repeated on the mosaic from Cuicul described above p. 115.

You may ask why the girl revealing the liknon tries to hold her back. The mystae do not fear her any more, she may remain with them, but she has done her service, she is bound to vanish. The mystae should not be reminded of the gloomy side of the mystery teaching. Joy begins.

If the above interpretation of the great fresco in the Villa Item is right we have an actual illustration of the terrifying apparitions which, according to the testimony of Celsus, were introduced in the Bacchic mysteries. They gave a chill of horror to the initiation and made salvation appear the more blissful. This was the culminating rite of the mysteries, the purpose of which was the assurance of a happy afterlife. The daemonic woman is no masked figure, she is as is usual transposed into a mythical figure; in the mystery rites her part was played by some masked mysta. After she had vanished and the mystae were sure of their fate, the joyful part of the feast could begin, a mitigated imitation of the Bacchic revelry which the Afterlife would bring.

The god of the Bacchic mysteries at Lerna, at Troizen, and of the Herois at Delphi was Dionysos who descended to the Underworld and ascended, bringing with him his mother to Olympus; and the child, killed by the Titans and reborn, is hinted at in the two descents of the Rhodian inscription. This may seem to be the best example of an idea, dear to scholars who tried to find a common background of beliefs in the mysteries of the Roman age, that is, that the death and resurrection of the god was the prototype of the death and resurrection of man; thus the mystae would be sure of rising again from death. But this is not so. The adherents of the Bacchic mysteries did not believe that they would rise up from the dead; they believed that they would lead a life of eternal bliss and joy in the Other World. This life is graphically described in a remarkable Latin inscription from Philippi.[36] "While we, overcome by our loss, are in misery, you in peace and once more restored live in the Elysian fields" . . . (The reading and interpretation of the other lines quoted are disputable, but the text clearly speaks of the dead boy as having been welcomed either by tattooed Maenads or by the Naiads.) It is pictured after the pattern of the myths, and so are the representations on the sarcophagi. We see on them Dionysos and Ariadne, or Dionysos in a car drawn by panthers, surrounded by the Bacchic thiasus (maenads, Satyrs, Silenus), or the Indian triumph of Dionysos. It is not to be believed that Roman adherents of the Bacchic mysteries thought much of the child killed by the Titans and reborn or of Dionysos carrying up Semele from the Underworld; most of them were

---

36 [*tu placidus dum nos cr*]*uciamur volnere victi*
et reparatus item vivis in Elysiis

. . . .
nunc seu te Bromio signatae mystides ad se
florigere in prato congregant in satyrum,
sive canistriferae poscunt sibi Naides aequum,
qui ducibus taedis agmina festa trahas.

(l. 3 *ad se*, the stone has *aise*) Bücheler, Carmina epigraphica, 1233; Perdrizet, Cultes et mythes du Pangée, 1910, p. 96; cf. my GGR, ii, p. 350.

probably content with the Dionysos of the common myth. The representations on the sarcophagi offer an idealized and mythological image of the Bacchic revelry which the mystae expected in the Other Life, and there was probably something like it in the performances of the mystery assemblies. A late author speaks of melodies and dances in the Bacchic mysteries, adding that thus the perturbation of the ignorant is cleared away with play and joy.[37]

The Other Life was pictured as a Bacchic revelry. This quite materialistic conception was, as Cumont says,[38] not very elevated and the sensual pleasures promised to the initiated ones do not seem to be of a high character, but the masses were for a long time inclined to it, he says. The pleasures of Aphrodite were certainly not absent from the picture. Some sarcophagi present scenes of an amazing obscenity.[39]

Death is a mighty source of religion and religious belief. Man fears death instinctively and wonders what will befall him after death, and his anxiety is increased by moral self-consciousness, as old Kephalos says in Plato. The Bacchic mysteries owed their popularity in the Roman age to the answer they gave to this deep-seated anxiety. They calmed the fears and smoothed over the anxiety, they promised the bliss of an eternal banquet. They were convenient for easy-going people who wanted to be freed from qualms.

The cult of Dionysos was very widespread in the Roman empire and is especially prominent in the provinces in which Dionysos was fused with indigenous gods, Africa and Pannonia. Its frequency in Thrace and the neighbouring districts depended of course on old traditions. Generally the inscriptions inform us

---

[37] Aristides Quintilianus, de musica, iii, 25, p. 93 Jahn, διὸ καὶ τὰς βακχικὰς τελετὰς καὶ ὅσαι ταύταις παραπλήσιοι λόγου τινὸς ἔχεσθαί φασι, ὅπως ἂν ἡ τῶν ἀμαθεστέρων πτοίησις διὰ βίον ἢ τύχην ὑπὸ τῶν ἐν ταύταις μελῳδιῶν τε καὶ ὀρχήσεων ἅμα παιδιαῖς ἐκκαθαίρηται. The last words are reminiscent of what Plato says of the Orpheotelestae, de rep., ii, p. 364 E.

[38] Cumont, Les religions orientales, 4th ed., p. 203.

[39] Cumont, op. cit., p. 311, n. 65, quotes Müller-Wieseler, Denkmäler der alten Kunst, ii, pl. xliv, No. 548; Reinach, Répertoire etc., iii, 69, 6; cf. Anthologia latina, ed. Riese, 319.

only of its existence and at most of associations and their functionaries. This is not the place to enter into this vast subject.[40]
I want only to point to two publications which show that the
Bacchic ideas of the Afterlife had penetrated the northern provinces.

One is a tombstone found at a place in Bulgaria not far from
Sofia and published by Egger.[41] The reliefs are poor and the
Latin inscription very difficult to read and to understand. According to the editor's interpretation the stone is set up for a
woman who at the age of ten years was initiated into the mysteries of Dionysos, became a servant of the local god (*domni
Biacusti at(t)censita*), died twenty-three years later and joined
the thiasus of the god (*excitor ia[m] savis* [i. e. σάβοι, the Thra-
cian name of the followers of the god], *Filina comite matre* [the
priestess], *Nisi ancilla* [servant of Nysius, i. e. Dionysos]). The
relief on the top of the stone is interpreted as showing the
woman, accompanied by the priestess, being introduced to the
god.[42]

The other publication is a paper by Alföldi[43] treating some
funereal cars found in tombs in Belgica, Germania, Pannonia,
and Thrace. This mode of sepulture is indigenous, but that the
cars are ornamented especially with Bacchic emblems shows that
the men, carried to their tombs in these cars, and their people
believed in the happy afterlife promised by the Bacchic
mysteries.

---

[40] For a survey see A. Bruhl, Liber pater, 1953, pp. 213 ff.; the associations
pp. 268 ff.

[41] R. Egger, Der Grabstein von Čekančeva, Österreichische Akad. d. Wiss.,
Schriften der Balkankommission, Antiquarische Abt., xi: 2, 1950.

[42] I pass over the other symbols, referring to the editor. For the detached head
see also P. Lambrechts, L'exaltation de la tête dans la pensée et l'art des Celtes,
1954.

[43] A. Alföldi, Chars funéraires bacchiques dans les provinces occidentales de
l'empire romain, L'Antiquité classique viii, 1939, pp. 349 ff.

IX. Orphic and Pythagorean Influence.

In the previous chapters we have seen that the Bacchic mysteries had holy books, scrolls, from which something was recited to the mystae. We do not know what they contained, but it would only be natural if they had taken over suitable and selected parts from the vast amount of Orphic literature. Dionysos had a prominent part in Orphism. The banquet of the dead, that old and inveterate idea of a happy afterlife, was part of the Orphic doctrine.[1] Orphism had a recrudescence in the Hellenistic age, as is known from Egypt (above p. 12), and Alexandrian scholars collected the Orphic literature. At the end of Antiquity the Orphic poems were the Bible of the Neoplatonists. Pythagoreanism too had a recrudescence; we may point to Nigidius Figulus, and to various Neo-Pythagorean tracts in Doric dialect, and scholars have tried to show that the imagery of the wonderful subterranean basilica near Porta Maggiore from the first century A. D. is inspired by Pythagorean doctrines.[2] In this age Orphism and Pythagoreanism went together. Since the Roman Bacchic mysteries are known only through the monuments, we cannot expect to find traces of such an influence, and if it existed the adherents had certainly selected such parts as were convenient to them and passed over others, probably, for example, the dismemberment of the child Dionysos by the Titans.

Very interesting is a recently published inscription from Smyrna which gives valuable information concerning the contents of the mysteries, and is the more valuable as it comes from a Greek city.[3] When Heberdey copied it the stone was in a private collection at Smyrna; it is now in the museum at Leiden.

---

[1] This is well known, see e. g. Cumont, Symbolisme funéraire, pp. 372 ff.

[2] J. Carcopino, La basilique pythagoricienne de la Porte Majeure, 1927.

[3] J. Keil, Inschriften aus Smyrna, Anzeiger d. österreich. Akad. Wien, xc, 1953, pp. 16 ff. No. 1; LSAM, 84.

The inscription is written in good letters of the second century A. D. and is composed in hexameters. It was set up by a man whose name is lost except the ending -της, son of Menandros. He styles himself θεοφάντης. We come back to this title below (p. 138). The editor suggests (p. 18) that the inscription comes from the sanctuary of Dionysos Breiseus which was situated outside the town, for we know that mysteries were attached to this old cult in the Roman age.[4] This is possible, but by no means certain,

<pre>
. . . . -της Μενάνδρου ὁ θεοφάντης ἀνέθηκεν.
[πάν]τες ὅσοι τέμενος Βρομίου ναούς τε περᾶτε,
τεσσαράκοντα μὲν ἤματα ἀπ' ἐχθέσεως πεφύλαχθε
νηπιάχοιο βρέφους, μὴ δὴ μήνειμα γένηται,
5 ἔκτρωσίν τε γυναικὸς ὁμοίως ἤματα τόσσα·
ἢν δέ τιν' οἰκείων θάνατος καὶ μοῖρα καλύψῃ,
εἴργεσθαι μηνὸς τρίτατον μέρος ἐκ προπύλοιο·
ἢν δ' ἀπ' ἀλλοτρίων οἴκων τι μίασμα γένηται,
ἠελίους τρισσοὺς μεῖναι νέκυος φθιμένοιο,
10 μηδὲ μελανφάρους προσί αι βωμοῖσιν ἄνακτ[ος]
μηδ' ἀθύτοις θυσίαις ἱερῶν ἐπὶ χεῖρας ἰάλ[λειν]
μηδ' ἐν βακχείοις ὠὸν ποτὶ δαῖτα τ[ίθεσθαι]
καὶ κραδίην καρποῦν ἱεροῖς βωμοῖς [ἀλέασθαι]
ἠδὲ ὀσμοῦ τ' ἀπέχεσθαι, ὃν ΔΗΓ. . . . . .
15 ἐχθροτάτην ῥίζαν κυάμων ἐκ σπε. . . . . . .
Τειτάνων προλέγειν μύσταις . . . .
καὶ καλάμοισι κροτεῖν οὐ θέσ[μιον εἶναι]
ἤμασιν οἷς μύσται θυσί[ας . . . . . .
[μηδ]ὲ φορεῖν συ. . . . .
</pre>

After the preamble the text begins by prescribing the periods of time which must elapse before anyone who has contracted an impurity is allowed to enter the sanctuary of the god, here called Bromios. The first of these prescriptions is remarkable and recurs only in the sacral law from Ptolemais in upper Egypt:[5] if anyone has exposed a child, the time prescribed is forty days, the longest period ever mentioned and as long as that prescribed for a woman who has miscarried (v. 5). The editor asks (p. 18 n. 4) if this is due to a condemnation of this usage, which was common in ancient times. One may also refer to the increasing love

---

[4] See above pp. 47 f.
[5] G. Plaumann, Ptolemais in Oberägypten, 1930, pp. 54 ff.

of children in the Roman age, but I think that there is a more special reason. Small children, even babies, were in this age initiated into the Bacchic mysteries. Whoever exposed a child deprived it of the boon of a happy afterlife, promised even to children by the Dionysiac mysteries. Perhaps the crime of the Titans against the child Dionysos (cf. below p. 138) lurks in the background. The following lines, vv. 6–9, prescribe the usual periods for anyone who has come into contact with a death in his family, the third part of a month, or if elsewhere, three days.

The editor makes the pertinent remark (p. 19) that the periods usually prescribed after sexual intercourse are missing. This is perhaps not accidental. The pleasures of Aphrodite were not absent from the happy afterlife promised to the Bacchic mystae and they may not have been averse to them in this life.

The most interesting part of this inscription is the following lines which contain certain prescriptions especially referring to the mystery cult. It is a pity that precisely these lines are mutilated at the end, but the sense is clear in most of them. The editor rightly mentions Orphic influence, but there is also a Pythagorean influence. Pythagoreanism and Orphism went together in this age.

The first of these prescriptions, v. 10, not to approach the altars of the god in black clothes (μελανφάρους), needs no comment. Black was the colour of sorrow and the mysteries ought to be a joyous feast.

V. 11. μηδ' ἀθύτοις θυσίαις ἱερῶν ἐπὶ χῖρας ἰάλ[λειν. The editor's supplement seems certain because of the allusion to a Homeric phrase. This line and the following give prescriptions for the sacred meal. Sacred meals were a part of other mysteries too,[6] e. g. those of Mithras. It may be surmised that they were not much more than a plentiful dinner to the mystae of Bacchus, who were fond of the pleasures of life. The prescriptions seem to aim at preventing such a desacralization. The word ἀθυτος may signify either "what has not been sacrificed" or "what is not allowed to be sacrificed". If the former sense is

---

[6] Cf. Cumont, Gaionas, le δειπνοκρίτης, Compte-rendu de l'Acad. des inscriptions, 1917, pp. 275 ff.

preferred it is forbidden to begin the meal until the dishes have been sacrificed, i. e. devoted to god, sacralized. If the latter sense is preferable, the sentence refers to the following prohibitions of certain food stuffs.[7] In any case the sacred character of the meal is stressed against misuses which might be feared. The interesting result is that our knowledge of the Dionysiac mysteries is enriched by the fact that they comprised a sacral meal.

In line 12, μηδ' ἐν Βαχχείοις ᾠὸν ποτὶ δαῖτα τ[ίθεσθαι. the mysteries are called Baccheia and the meal is expressly mentioned. It is forbidden to serve an egg at the sacred meal. Eggs are mentioned among the foods prohibited by the Pythagoreans,[8] but this prohibition has a deeper ground in Orphic doctrine. The Bacchic mysteries had taken over the cosmic egg from Orphism and it was sacred to them because, as Plutarch says, it was an imitation of that which produces and in itself encloses all.[9] As it was highly venerated by the mystae of Dionysos it ought not to be served and eaten, although it was otherwise a common and well-liked food.

The following three lines refer to Pythagorean customs. V. 13, καὶ κραδίην καρποῦν ἱεροῖς βωμοῖς... A negative word must be supplemented, e. g. ἀλέασθαι. καρποῦν signifies "burn".[10] A much-quoted Pythagorean sentence forbade eating the heart,[11] much less ought it to be offered to the god himself. One may perhaps be reminded of the myth that Athena saved the heart of the child Dionysos and brought it to Zeus.

---

[7] Cf. the Pythagorean prescription: Θυσίμων χρὴ ἐσθίειν μόνον, Aristotle in Iamblichus, vita Pythag. 85.

[8] In the review of the Pythagorean prohibitions in Diogenes Laertius, viii, 33, together with certain fish, animals which lay eggs, beans. Also in the scholion on the Haloa to Lucianus, dial. mer, vii, published by Rohde, Rhein. Mus. xxv. 1870, pp. 558 ff. (p. 279, 24 Rabe; reprinted by Deubner, Attische Feste, p. 61, n. 5). It concerns a women's festival localized in Eleusis, but the origin is certainly Pythagorean. Plenty of food is served except such as is prohibited by the mystics (ἐν τῷ μυστικῷ): pomegranates, apples, fowl, eggs, and certain fish.

[9] See below pp. 140.

[10] P. Stengel, Opferbräuche der Griechen, pp. 166 ff.

[11] See F. Boehm, De symbolis Pythagoreis, Diss. Berlin 1905, pp. 23 f. with references.

Vv. 14 ff. ΗΔΕΟΣΜΟΥ τ' ἀπέχεσθαι, ὃν ΔΗΓ — — —
          ἐχθροτάτην ῥίζαν κύαμον ἐκ σπε — — — —
To try to supplement these verses is of no use. The supplement
of the editor σπέ[ρματος] is very dubious. He takes the two
verses to form one sentence but even this may be doubted. He
takes the word ὀσμός to signify "smell" (p. 20) and says that he
does not understand its reference. In my previous paper, quoted
above p. 3, I mentioned that Professor Wifstrand pointed out
that the word ὀσμός is extremely rare, occurring only once in an
addendum to the Herbarium of Dioscurides,[12] where it is said
to designate the same plant as μήδιον. As this is a leguminous
plant like the bean, it seemed reasonable that this too was
prohibited by the Pythagoreans. The phrase "the most odious
root of the beans" is, according to Professor Wifstrand, only a
poetical metaphrasis, and this seems to be so. However, in an
article, which will appear during 1957 in the Bulletin de corres-
pondence hellénique and of which he has kindly sent me a copy,
Director Daux proposes a new interpretation of the obscure
letters ΗΔΕΟΣΜΟΥ. He reads ἡδεοσμοῦ, viz. ἡδυοσμοῦ, the mint.
The Director of the Dictionary of Modern Greek, Kalléris, has
pointed out to him that this word, written ἡδεοσμοῦ, is found
in two papyri of the sixth and seventh centuries A. D. (Sammel-
buch griech. Urkunden aus Ägypten, 4483 and 4485), a vulgar
form of ἡδυοσμοῦ. Mr Kalléris adds that today mint is always
used as a condiment of beans. Again I have consulted Professor
Wifstrand. He says that the example, Anthol. pal., xi, 413,
ὤκιμον, ἡδύοσμον, πήγανον, ἀσπαραγός, is not relevant. The
υ is read as a consonant, a phenomenon of which there are earlier
instances, while in our inscription ἡδεοσμοῦ implies a synizesis.
Moreover he observes that the word in our inscription is mascu-
line, while elsewhere it is neuter where the gender can be
discerned. However, this is of less relevance, and he is of the
opinion that the examples adduced from the papyri are conclusive
and prefers the explanation proposed by Daux. I agree with him.

---

[12] Dioscurides, II § 147; in the latest edition by Wellmann I, p. 213, ὀσμηρός
is conjectured. This will be the reason why the word is left out in the latest
edition of Liddell and Scott.

What is left of v. 16, Τειτάνων προλέγειν μύσταις — — —, is clear, although the end is missing. Something is to be expounded to the mystae about the Titans. This cannot be anything but their crime against the child Dionysos. It is extremely important to know that this main myth of Orphism was taken over by the Dionysiac mysteries in the Roman age, although, of course, we are not entitled to conclude that it was part of them everywhere. This lends some colour to the information that dances performed by Titans, Corybants, Satyrs, and Boukoloi were popular in Asia Minor.[13]

Lines 17 and 18, καὶ καλάμοισι κροτεῖν οὐ θέσ[μιον — —, ἤμασιν οἷς μύσται θυσι — — —, seem less important. It is forbidden to use reeds as castanets, which happened sometimes.[14] The mystae had to use other instruments of a similar kind. On the great painting in the Villa Item a nude dancing girl clashes cymbals over her head. Only a few letters are left of the last line. We cannot tell whether the inscription continued or not.

The discussion of the title θεοφάντης, which the priest who set up the inscription gives to himself, has been deferred until now. This word and others like it are well known.[15] ἱεροφάντης is the oldest of them. It designated the highest functionary of the Eleusinian mysteries, who showed the ἱερά, the holy things, and was the leader of the mysteries. Accordingly the words ὀργιοφάντης, τελεσιφάντης were coined. The concrete significance is a little obscured in these words, for the orgia are not objects. The ὀργιοφάντης is the man who performs the rites of the orgia. The word σεβαστοφάντης, which was coined in the so-called mysteries devoted to the emperor in the Roman age, can be understood as meaning that he showed an image of the emperor to the mystae, and the word θεοφάντης likewise; this would mean that the man showed an image of the god, i. e. Dionysos.

I think that this is hardly likely. We do not hear of any such ceremony in these mysteries, but, having regard to our scanty

---

13 See above p. 60.
14 Schol. Aristoph. Nubes, v. 260, quoted by the editor, l. c. p. 20, n. 7.
15 Quoted by Keil, l. c. p. 18, n. 3.

knowledge of them, this is not decisive. However, I am inclined to suggest that the θεοφάντης as well as the σεβαστοφάντης showed the power of the god Dionysos or the emperor respectively by praising them, their power, and their deeds in words. We know the ὑμνῳδοί in the cult of the emperor in Asia Minor, associations of prominent men who sang hymns in honour of the emperor. As to Dionysos we read in the Orphic hymnbook, which certainly emanated from some mystery cult, probably at Pergamon, ten hymns to Dionysos, more than to any other god.[16] In the mysteries of Dionysos Kathegemon at Pergamon a ὑμνοδι-δάσκαλος appears. Such hymns were a constant element of the cults of this age. The part of the θεοφάντης was that of a θεολόγος, as those are called who preach the god's virtues.[17]

The explanation of the title θεοφάντης may be, says Keil (p. 18 n. 3), that the god has to announce himself, but he adds that it is not certain if we may conclude from the title that the priest appeared in the role of the god and announced something to the mystae in sacred ceremonies. In certain Bacchic associations, at least in that of the Iobacchi in Athens, the members played the role of some gods;[18] we may also remember the Bacchic dances which were very popular in Asia Minor.

These Smyrnaean mysteries are an exceptional case and we are not entitled to generalize their prescriptions, much less to take them as valid for the Bacchic mysteries in Italy. But it is important that the central doctrine of Orphism, the crime of the Titans against the child Dionysos, was taught here and that so many Pythagorean prescriptions in regard to food were adopted. Finally this is the only text in which a sacred meal is mentioned, but this is certainly mere chance. The meal was a matter of course which did not need mention.

Eggs were a prohibited food to the Pythagoreans. The reason may be that the egg was a common offering to the dead. I have

---

[16] See above p. 59.

[17] See my GGR, ii, pp. 362 f. In the mysteries of Demeter at Smyrna two sisters are mentioned as θεολόγοι, ibid. p. 340; a θεολογία in the statutes of the Iobacchi above p. 59.

[18] See above pp. 60 f.

treated this topic long ago.[19] Much more could be added, but I
call attention only to some Apulian vases, recently published.[20]
On an Apulian amphora a crater is seen standing between two
eggs in a naïskos, and on the stairs supporting the tomb monument another crater and a number of eggs are disposed. On one
of the two Gnathia vases[21] a table is seen on which are two
craters and between them an egg, while at either side of the
table is a torch. The other shows two eggs and between them
an alabastron.

In Orphism the egg had a deeper sense, it was the cosmic egg
from which the world and everything in it originate. The Bacchic mysteries took over this idea. Plutarch and an author
about three centuries later, Macrobius, mention it, and their
wording is such as to refer to Bacchic mysteries of their own
time. Plutarch first refers to the holy Orphic tale that the egg is
older than the hen and comprises in itself the seniority of the
birth of all; he keeps silence concerning the rest because it is
mystic and goes on to say that everything comes forth from an
egg, listing a series of animals, and ends: "it is not odd for it to be
sacred to those who partake in the Dionysiac mysteries as an imitation of that which produces and in itself encloses all."[22]
Macrobius says: "that it may not seem that I have exalted the
egg too much through the word 'element', ask those who are
initiated into the *sacra* of Liber pater, among whom the egg is
venerated so much that it is called an image of the world
(*mundus*) because of its round and nearly spherical shape, shut
up in all directions and within itself enclosing life; and as
all men agree, the *mundus* is the principle of the universe."[23]

---

[19] Das Ei im Totenkult der Alten, Archiv f. Religionswissenschaft, xi, 1908,
pp. 539 ff., reprinted with some additions in my Opuscula selecta, i, pp. 3 ff.,
addendum, ii, p. 1057.

[20] By K. Schauenburg, Archäol. Jahrbuch, lxviii, 1953, p. 62, fig. 17; p. 63,
fig. 18; p. 64, fig. 19.

[21] Gnathia, from which this class of vases has its name, is a town in Apulia.

[22] Plutarch, quaest. conviv., p. 636 D et seq., ὅθεν οὐκ ἀπὸ τρόπου τοῖς περὶ
τὸν Διόνυσον ὀργιασμοῖς ὡς μίμημα τοῦ τὰ πάντα γεννῶντος καὶ περιέχοντος ἐν
ἑαυτῷ συγκαθωσίωται.

[23] Macrobius, Saturnalia, vii, 16, 8, *et ne videar plus nimio extulisse ovum*

Fig. 37. *Painting in a columbarium near the Villa Pamfilia in Rome.*

This is plainly the cosmic egg from which the world sprang
forth. I called attention to a painting in the columbarium
near the Villa Pamfilia in Rome in which five young men
are seen looking at certain objects on the table before them,
three eggs[24] (Fig. 37). The scene is commonly explained by a
reference to the old question whether the egg or the hen is
older. The eggs are divided lengthwise in an upper light-coloured
and a lower dark-coloured half. They are thought of as the
cosmic egg which split, the upper part becoming the heaven

---

elementi vocabulo, consule initiatos sacris Liberi patris, in quibus hac veneratione
ovum colitur, ut ex forma tereti ac paene sphaerali atque undique versum clausa
et includente intra se vitam mundi simulacrum vocetur, mundum autem consensu
omnium constat universitatis esse principium. P. Boyancé, Une allusion à l'oeuf
orphique, Mélanges d'archéologie et d'histoire de l'école française de Rome, lii,
1935, pp. 1 ff., takes up this subject in a learned paper. Starting from the passages
quoted he explains a passage in Martianus Capella, ii, 109 et seq., in which the
egg contains the drink of immortality. His attempt to explain *mundus* in the
quoted passage of Macrobius as Aion is not convincing. The vases from South
Italy discussed pp. 16 ff. are a supplement to the materials collected in my
paper, Das Ei etc.

[24] In my paper, Das Ei etc., p. 543, in the reprint p. 17.

and the lower part the earth.[25] Plutarch gives the answer to the question according to the Orphic doctrine: the egg is older than the hen.

Cosmic ideas were not foreign to the mysteries of the Roman age, but it may be doubted whether they were sufficient to give such a prominent place to the egg in the Bacchic mysteries, whose adherents perhaps were not particularly interested in speculative ideas. Eggs, even made of clay and painted, are often found in tombs, and according to Juvenal an egg was a regular offering to the dead.[26] This custom had a deeper sense than a mere offering of food. The egg is always, even in modern folklore, conceived of as enclosing life-power; it looks like a dead thing, a stone, but life proceeds miraculously from it. As Plutarch says, it seems to enclose and produce all and therefore it seems to be the origin of all, the cosmic egg, and as Macrobius says, it encloses life. Life is what the dead lack and the egg was most appropriate to restore life to them.

It may be asked whether the use of the phallus as the principal symbol of the Bacchic mysteries might be better understood under this aspect. It was, of course, taken over from the many phallic processions and monuments in Greek cult which made it appear as the peculiar characteristic of the cult of Dionysos. It was shocking to the Roman feeling of decency, not so to the Greeks, but the Romans had been hellenized in this age.[27] But the prominent place of the phallus would be better understood if it had a deeper significance. The generative organ confers life;[28] like the egg it contains the life-power which the dead lack and need. Therefore it was set up on tombs.[29] Like the

---

[25] See the paper quoted in the foregoing note.

[26] Juvenal, v, v. 84. Cf. above p. 139.

[27] Cf. Festugière, loc. cit. (above p. 2 n. 5), p. 208.

[28] This is the interpretation of the Neoplatonists. Jamblichus, de mysteriis, i, 11, τὴν μὲν τῶν φαλλῶν στάσιν τοῦ γονίμου δυνάμεως σύνθημά τί φαμεν καὶ ταύτην προσκαλεῖσθαι νομίζομεν εἰς τὴν γενεσιουργίαν τοῦ κόσμου. Its use in fertility rites is known, e. g. from the rites of the Thesmophoria as described in the scholia in Lucianum, p. 276, l. 14 ff. Rabe; it referred also to human fertility, ibid. p. 279, l. 24 ff.; both are reprinted in Deubner, Attische Feste, p. 40 n. 5 and p. 61 n. 5 resp.

[29] See above pp. 44 f.

egg it may have been a symbol of life-power and life. Since our knowledge of the Bacchic mysteries is so scanty we cannot be sure that they did not have other symbols unknown to us — the egg does not appear on the monuments —, but the fact is that the liknon was their most prominent and the phallus their most conspicuous symbol. I think that the above suggestion is neither unfounded nor unlikely.

X. Conclusion

The Religious and the Social Aspects

The Dionysiac or Bacchic mysteries — these are two names of the same cult, and I have used them only to distinguish between its Greek and its Roman aspects — are purely Greek. They have no trace of Oriental influence. They have taken over some paraphernalia of the old orgia: the thyrsus, the tympana, the torch. On works of art their celebration has, as usual, been transferred into the mythical sphere, the partakers being represented as Maenads, Satyrs, and Silenus. Not without reference to the old processions in which phalli were carried, they have created or appropriated a new emblem which became their chief symbol, the liknon filled with fruit among which a phallus rises. The meaning attributed to this symbol can only be guessed at. It must have had a deeper sense, or it would not have become their paramount sign. They also took over the common symbol of all mysteries, the cista mystica.

They had doctrines. Lectures were delivered from holy books to the mystery assemblies, as the Roman monuments show. As to Greece and Asia Minor the inscriptions are silent with two exceptions. A sermon was preached to the Iobacchi, and at Smyrna something was recited to the mystae concerning the Titans. There Pythagorean food restrictions were also imposed. The chief doctrine was, at least in Italy, that of an Afterlife of punishments and bliss. The horrors are recorded not only in

Roman works of art but also by the explicit words of Celsus and Plutarch. The bliss in the Afterlife was the Bacchic revel represented in accordance with the mythology, but originally it was an old idea that had been taken up also by the Orphics. Orphic ideas may in some measure have determined their ideas of the Afterlife, although they were common. Orphic influence is evident in regard to the cosmogonic egg, a philosophical myth which Plutarch and Macrobius ascribe to the mystae of Dionysos.

The Dionysiac mysteries certainly varied from place to place and from time to time. The space in time is about half a millennium and the geographical space extends from Asia Minor, Thrace, and Egypt to Italy and Africa. It is not possible to make out a general pattern, as has been done for the Oriental mysteries. The varieties are conditioned by the fact that the Dionysiac mysteries were connected with old Greek cults that had various forms, while in Asia Minor they were sometimes grafted on old cults each with its own peculiarities, not to speak of the actors' and dancers' associations that posed as mysteries. In Italy they seem to be more homogeneous, if the representations do not deceive us. This may be due to the fact that ancient cults of the Greek Dionysos were lacking in this country.

The Dionysiac mysteries brought nothing new in the religious sphere, neither in rites nor in beliefs. The elements were old; even the liknon, the chief symbol of the Roman mysteries, was a combination of old elements. The titles and the names of the members and functionaries in the Greek inscriptions are drawn from old sources, only now they are prodigiously developed. The belief in the Afterlife with its punishing daemons and with the bliss of an eternal banquet was common although tinged with Bacchic elements. And even if at times something was taken over from Orphism, Orphism too came from an earlier age.

I have called attention to the fact that the monuments, through which we know the Bacchic mysteries in Italy, were commissioned by well-to-do people. The man who had the glorious fresco in the Villa Item painted and he who had the Villa Farnesina decorated with so many paintings and stucco reliefs must have been wealthy; so too the owner of the "Homeric" house with its underground rooms and paintings. The Campana reliefs were not made for poor people. The sculptured sarcophagi were expensive, only well-to-do people could afford such luxury for their final repose. We know less about the social conditions of the adherents of the Dionysiac mysteries in Greece and Asia Minor. But the Iobacchi in Athens, who though not called mystae so nearly resemble a Dionysiac mystery association that they have often been adduced in expounding the mysteries, were people of gentle birth: their head was a son or grandson of the famous Herodes Atticus. The members of the mystery association of Dionysos Kathegemon in Pergamon were prominent citizens, and the actors who formed other mystery associations in Asia Minor were no mean people. However, many inscriptions give no information in regard to the social status of the mystae.

That wine-drinking and banqueting had a large place in the Dionysiac mystery associations is self-evident. In this age Dionysos was considered the god of wine and especially of intoxication. On the other hand there was less occasion for the inscriptions to mention and the monuments to represent this side of the celebration; but in mythical guise intoxication is often seen. However, the association at Apollonia in Thrace has among its functionaries a wine steward and a "maître de cuisine". The Roman monuments often show mixing and drinking vessels.

For the banquets couchs were needed, στιβάς, Latin *stibadium*. They are mentioned, e. g. in the statutes of the Iobacchi and in a Pergamene inscription. Two inscriptions from Rome say that the *stibadium* had been restored in its place: it seems to have been a permanent construction. In Greece it was perhaps sometimes an architectural construction. In Greece the mystae had sometimes a house called Baccheion for their assemblies. We do not hear of these in Italy, where the mysteries seem to have been celebrated in private houses. It is commonly assumed that the hall with the great fresco in the Villa Item and the large underground room in the "Homeric" house were destined for such celebrations, probably also some room or other in the Villa Farnesina. If the Bacchic mysteries in Italy were

10

celebrated in private houses of well-to-do people, this is perhaps the reason why inscriptions referring to them are lacking. The master and the mistress of the house arranged the celebration as they liked. There was no hierarchy, no functionaries elected for a certain time who desired to commemorate themselves. In this respect the similarity with the earliest Christians is undeniable, as is true also of the admission of children. But caution is needed because we have no direct testimonies. Perhaps one may ask why small temples were decorated with terracotta reliefs representing mystery scenes, if, that is, the supposition is correct that the Campana reliefs were destined for temples as well as for houses. But this too is uncertain.

This is the other side of the Dionysiac mysteries, which gave a large place to drinking and eating, feasting and rejoicing. It may have been excused by the fact that their god, Dionysos, was the god of wine and of joy. His devotees yielded also to sensualism. The sexual symbols of the cult were certainly not, as among simple people, thought of merely as bringers of fertility; for the well-to-do townspeople they had a piquant attraction, allowed by the rites, even if not so crude as the Carmina Priapea. The oft-represented mythical companions of Dionysos, the Satyrs and Maenads, imply not a little of sensualism, and the picture of the Afterlife seems not to have been free from it. On the other hand the sentimental love of children in this age caused even children to be admitted to the Bacchic mysteries and to the Bacchic Elysium. The Bacchic mysteries were not, like other mysteries, secret in the strict sense; otherwise we should not have so many representations of the rites, which of course often, but not always, were transferred into the mythical sphere.

The mysteries of Dionysos appealed to well-to-do people who loved a pleasant and luxurious life. The banquet of the blessed Dead appealed to the taste of a public that was fond of the pleasures of life and did not take religion too seriously. The mysteries of Dionysos appealed to people who from education and conservatism kept to the old culture and religion and yielded less easily to the lure of the more demanding foreign religions, but who still wanted a little thrill of religion as a spice to the daily routine.

These characteristics explain the popularity of the Bacchic mysteries among the well-to-do classes, and they explain also why they have left so few traces, except for inscriptions and monuments, in the history of late paganism. These people were not in earnest about religion.

The creation of new Dionysiac mysteries in the Hellenistic age and their popularity in Roman times, the attachment of their adherents to the enjoyments of life, their belief in a happy afterlife, their love of children, these and the colouring of Orphic and mystic ideas all shed an interesting light on the mentality of the age. They are the only new mysteries of Greek origin which spread widely, and although much less noticed by scholars than the Oriental cults they seem to have been more popular than their rivals among the upper classes. But apparently there was at the same time a weakness in their content, which made them unable to compete in real influence with those more earnest and exacting mysteries.

INDEX

ANCIENT RELIGION AND MYTHOLOGY

An Arno Press Collection

Altmann, Walter. **Die Römischen Grabaltäre der Kaiserzeit** (The Roman Grave Altars of Imperial Times). 1905

Amandry, Pierre. **La Mantique Apollinienne à Delphes** (Apollo's Oracle at Delphi). 1950

Appel, Georgius. **De Romanorum Precationibus** (Concerning the Prayers of the Romans). 1909

Bidez, Joseph and Franz Cumont. **Les Mages Hellénisés: Zoroastre, Ostanès et Hystaspe** (Hellenized Magi: Zoroaster, Ostanes and Hystaspes). Two volumes in one. 1938

Bouché-Leclercq, A[uguste]. **Les Pontifes de l'Ancienne Rome** (The Pontiffs of Ancient Rome). 1871

Cumont, Franz. **Recherches sur le Symbolisme Funéraire des Romains** (Investigations on the Funerary Symbolism of the Romans). 1942

Domaszewski, Alfred von. **Abhandlungen zur Römischen Religion** (Essays on Roman Religion). 1909

Domaszewski, Alfred von. **Die Religion des Römischen Heeres** (The Religion of the Roman Army). 1895

Edelstein, Emma J[eannette] and Ludwig Edelstein. **Asclepius: A Collection and Interpretation of the Testimonies.** Two volumes in one. 1945

Foucart, P[aul] [François]. **Des Associations Religieuses Chez les Grecs:** Thiases, Eranes, Orgéons (The Religious Associations of the Greeks: Thiasoi, Eranoi, Orgeones). 1873

Foucart, Paul [François]. **Les Mystères d'Éleusis** (The Mysteries of Eleusis). 1914

Gruppe, O[tto]. **Griechische Mythologie und Religionsgeschichte** (Greek Mythology and the History of Greek Religion). Two volumes. 1906

Harrison, Jane E[llen]. Prolegomena to the Study of Greek Religion. 1922

Jeanmaire, H[enri]. **Couroi et Courètes:** Essai sur l'Éducation Spartiate et sur les Rites d'Adolescence dans l'Antiquité Hellénique (Couroi and Couretes: Essay on Spartan Education and on the Rites of Adolescence in Greek Antiquity). 1939

De-Marchi, Attilio. **Il Culto Privato di Roma Antica** (The Private Cult in Ancient Rome). Two volumes in one. 1896/1903

Moulinier, Louis. **Le Pur et l'Impur dans la Pensée des Grecs d'Homère à Aristote** (The Pure and the Impure in the Thought of the Greeks from Homer to Aristotle). 1952

Nilsson, Martin P[ersson]. **The Dionysiac Mysteries of the Hellenistic and Roman Age.** 1957

Norden, Eduard. **Aus Altrömischen Priesterbüchern** (From the Books of the Ancient Roman Priests). 1939

Otto, Walter [Gustav Albrecht]. **Priester und Tempel im Hellenistischen Ägypten** Priest and Temple in Hellenistic Egypt). Two volumes in one. 1905/1908

Plutarch. **The Roman Questions of Plutarch.** Edited by H[erbert] J[ennings] Rose. 1924

Plutarch. **The Greek Questions of Plutarch.** With a New Translation and a Commentary by W. R. Halliday. 1928

Robert, Carl. **Archaeologische Hermeneutik** (The Interpretation of Archaeological Material). 1919

Robert, Carl. **Bild und Lied:** Archäologische Beiträge zur Geschichte der Griechischen Heldensage (Image and Song: Archaeological Contributions to the History of the Greek Hero Sagas). 1881

Roman Augury and Etruscan Divination. 1975.

Rouse, William Henry Denham. **Greek Votive Offerings:** An Essay in the History of Greek Religion. 1902

Scott, Kenneth. **The Imperial Cult Under the Flavians.** 1936

Stengel, Paul. **Die Griechischen Kultusaltertümer** (Antiquities Relating to Greek Cults). 1920

Tabeling, Ernst. **Mater Larum:** Zum Wesen der Larenreligion (Mother of the Lares: Towards the Essence of the Lares Religion). 1932

Tresp, Alois. **Die Fragmente der Griechischen Kultschriftsteller** (Fragments of the Writers on the Greek Cults). 1914

Two Studies on the Roman Pontifices. 1975

Varro, Marcus Terentius. **M. Terenti Varronis Antiquitatum Rerum Divinarum. Libri I, XIV, XV, XVI** (Marcus Terentius Varro's Books on Ancient Religious Matters). Edited by Reinholdo Agahd. 1898

Wissowa, Georg. **Gesammelte Abhandlungen zur Römischen Religions und Stadtgeschichte** (Collected Essays on Roman Religion and Political History). 1904